Spectacle of Empire

SPECTACLE OF EMPIRE

Marc Lescarbot's
Theatre of Neptune in New France

400th Anniversary Edition

Edited & Introduced by
JERRY WASSERMAN

Talonbooks
Vancouver

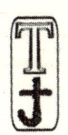

Typeset in Adobe Caslon and printed and bound in Canada.
Printed on 100% post-consumer recycled paper.

First Printing: 2006

The publisher gratefully acknowledges the financial support of the Canada Council for the Arts; the Government of Canada through the Book Publishing Industry Development Program; and the Province of British Columbia through the British Columbia Arts Council for our publishing activities.

Library and Archives Canada Cataloguing in Publication

Lescarbot, Marc, 1570?–1630?
    Spectacle of empire : Marc Lescarbot's Theatre of Neptune in New France / edited and introduced by Jerry Wasserman. — 400th anniversary commemorative ed.

Translation of: Théâtre de Neptune en la Nouvelle-France.
Text in French with English translations by Harriette Taber Richardson and Eugene and Renate Benson.
Also includes Ben Jonson's The masque of blackness (1605).
Includes bibliographical references.
ISBN 0-88922-547-8

    I. Wasserman, Jerry, 1945– II. Richardson, Harriette Taber
III. Benson, Eugene, 1928– IV. Benson, Renate, 1938– V. Jonson, Ben, 1573?–1637. Masque of blackness. VI. Title.

PQ1817.L652T5413 2006   842'.3   C2006-903665-9

ISBN-10: 0-88922-547-8
ISBN-13: 978-0-88922-547-3

Contents

Illustrations

❧ *Acknowledgements* ❧

Getting to Know Neptune

I visited Port Royal for the first time in May 2004 on a side-trip from Halifax, Nova Scotia, where my wife, Susan, and I were attending a conference on Canadian theatre. Standing on the shoreline of the Annapolis Basin in front of the small structure that is the restored Port Royal fort, staring out into the sheltered waters, I tried to envision exactly where the ship carrying the Sieur de Poutrincourt and Samuel de Champlain would have been anchored that November day four centuries ago; how Neptune, his Tritons, and the pretend-Indians in their canoes would have arranged themselves in relation to the larger vessel; and how anyone on the shore could possibly have heard any of the dialogue Marc Lescarbot wrote for the occasion. The spectacle was easier to imagine: the costumes, props, and gestures, the song and cannon fire. Thankfully, the rebuilt fort itself, the *Habitation*, is largely free of touristy tackiness (see fig. 1). In fact, though Port Royal is a Canadian National Historic Site, the *Habitation* was difficult to find—the signage in Annapolis Royal proper, about ten kilometres distant, where the former *British* fortress is very well preserved and promoted, was practically non-existent. Arriving there, we found a modest structure with few tourists, a ticket booth but no gift shop—we couldn't even buy a postcard on site—and only a single bilingual guide, in period costume, who gladly took us through the roughly furnished rooms, explaining who lived where and did what. When I asked him if he knew about the play, he responded by reciting Neptune's entire opening speech in French.

It was the kind of pilgrimage I had made before—finally standing in the place where it had all begun, the place where the plays and playwrights and theatre history I was teaching and writing about had actually originated. I had had similar experiences at Epidaurus and Stratford-upon-Avon, at the Comédie-Française, London's Royal Court, and Theatre Passe Muraille in Toronto. Growing up in New York, I had always had a feel for a certain kind of theatre. I knew viscerally what "Broadway" meant. "Off-Broadway" and

Fig. 1. Exterior view of the reconstructed Port Royal *Habitation*. Courtesy of *Wikipedia*. Photograph by Danielle Langlois.

"off off" became as familiar as drinking beer while I was going to college in the 1960s. But when I went on to graduate school, then started teaching, I realized that I felt fraudulent about a lot of what was supposedly "in my field." I felt uncomfortable claiming expertise in regard to material that arose out of particular geographies I had never experienced first-hand. Finally getting to those places, I have found, makes a big psychological difference.

As a latecomer to Canadian theatre, working in it as an actor and learning about it on the job as it became more and more my central academic focus in the 1970s and '80s, I was first convinced that nothing prior to 1967 really mattered much. That was when a homegrown, fully professionalized theatre had finally emerged in Canada with plays, playwrights, and a performance history sufficient to delineate some kind of canon. It was only in the mid-1990s, when I reluctantly inherited and began to teach a course in pre-1967 Canadian theatre history at the University of British Columbia, that I started to see the error of my ways. Canadian theatre, it turned out, has a history as full of incident, human interest, theatrical event, folly, heroism, and humour as any other nation's. As a hyphenated Ameri-Canadian, I developed a particular fascination with the long colonial struggle of Canada's pioneer theatre artists and entrepreneurs to carve out a newly defined, hybrid "Canadian" theatrical space amid the conflicting territories already occupied by British and American theatrical, political, and economic interests, while also negotiating across the nation's two internal solitudes: the French-English divide, and the even greater gap between First Nations and the Euro-Canadian settler-invader culture that came to dominate the northern half of the continent.

Marc Lescarbot's *The Theatre of Neptune in New France* was an exciting discovery for me. It was a starting point, an originary moment. We could talk in class about Native American and Native Canadian ritual performance, examine photographic reconstructions and artifacts, and even watch a video of authentic-looking (but staged) performances by Kwakwaka'wakw dancers in full regalia in Edward Curtis's 1914 film *In the Land of the Headhunters*. But when Eugene and Renate Benson published their new English translation of *The Theatre of Neptune* in 1982, and Anton Wagner reprinted it in his marvelous four-volume anthology, *Canada's Lost Plays*, we had an actual first *script* to read and study. Although recording a one-time-only event that had no apparent influence on the subsequent development of theatre in North America, *The Theatre of Neptune* was paradigmatic of a kind of performance that was more than just art or entertainment, though it was those things, too. It engaged political and cultural issues that were specific to North American colonial history but that remain current. It was exotic—a strange theatrical hybrid staged in boats on coastal waters—but it seemed to me also familiar somehow, connected to other plays I had read about and studied, and to the kinds of site-specific performances I was increasingly seeing in Vancouver. It adapted old world forms to new world circumstances, not unlike a much later landmark in Canadian theatre history, the opening of the Stratford Festival (see Wasserman 9). And it was really *old*. Who knew that we had a theatre history on our own soil that went back as far as Shakespeare's time? I found my students first bemused, then thrilled by the notion that they could trace the pedigree of the enterprise into which they were entering all the way back to 1606. It became the hook that snared them, and helped snare me.

Through it I discovered Lescarbot's *History of New France* and rediscovered Champlain's *Voyages*, a book I had known about since high school but hadn't looked at since then. But soon the Bensons' translation and *Canada's Lost Plays* went out of print. That was when I found that there had been earlier translations, including one (also out of print) by a remarkable American woman, Harriette Taber Richardson, who, it turned out, had been instrumental in arranging for the historical reconstruction of the fort which housed the men who wrote, designed, and performed the play. That place, in the same country but on the other side of the continent from where I lived, suddenly started becoming real to me. Then one day I realized that the four hundredth anniversary of the performance of *The Theatre of Neptune in New France* would soon be upon us. My brainstorm was to get the play back into print by November 2006 in an edition that would include the original French text, two of the English translations, each offering different kinds of valuable insights, and another dramatic work, in English, by a very well known playwright, contemporary with *The Theatre of Neptune* and with parallels to its art and politics that could help illuminate both texts. And I would contextualize it all, critically and historically, providing in Joseph Roach's term a "genealogy" of its performance (25–28), expanding on some of the excellent research previously published on these lesser-known forms: the nautical masque, the royal entry.

I owe great thanks to my publisher, Karl Siegler of Talonbooks, who not only agreed to my proposal but leapt at it with an enthusiasm that has inspired me. Thanks to Davinia Yip who kept the whip to me and shepherded this into print with her usual editorial precision and acuity. Thanks to my colleague Tony Dawson for his sharp critical eye and help, especially with Ben Jonson's arcane language. I'm grateful also to Eugene Benson, Denis Salter, and Ellen Mackay for their willingness to share ideas about the project. To Sue, for her patience and love. To the University of British Columbia's libraries and librarians for their extraordinary resources. To a host of international libraries and museums for their generosity in providing us with illustrations: Bibliotèque municipale de Rouen; Devonshire Collection, Chatsworth; Library and Archives Canada; Museum Plantin-Moretus, Antwerp; Pierpont Morgan Library, New York; Rare Book & Manuscript Library, University of Illinois, Urbana-Champagne. To Dominique Yupangco for her help with electronic images. And to my colleagues in the Association for Canadian Theatre Research and the students of UBC's Theatre 325 for always pushing me to get it right.

I dedicate this book to Patrick O'Neill. Enormously knowledgeable and generous, he knew more about the history of theatre in the Maritime provinces than I could ever learn in two lifetimes. Sadly, he didn't live to see this anniversary.

Jerry Wasserman
University of British Columbia

❧ *Introduction* ❧

Marc Lescarbot and the Spectacle of Empire

In November 1606, a tiny band of Frenchmen welcomed a small sailing ship into the sheltered waters of the North Atlantic harbour they had christened *Port-Royal*, in the land their king called *La Cadie* (a common aboriginal word for "place" ["Champlain Anniversary"]), later to become *l'Acadie* or Acadia. Aboard skiffs or canoes out on the water, a dozen of the men—some preparing to spend a third brutal winter in this distant outpost of France in the new world—honoured their returning countrymen by performing a play that, in an oblique way, would have reminded them of home. It enacted welcome and thanksgiving in an elaborate, small-scale spectacle of wishful imperial triumphalism. Its shipboard audience consisted of the colony's leader, Jean Biencourt, Sieur de Poutrincourt; the expedition's geographer/chronicler, Samuel de Champlain; and the ship's captain and crew. On shore, outside their fortified living quarters, others gathered: some to participate in the performance, some to help provide its special effects, the rest comprising a second important audience of colonists and local Mi'kmaq people, including their chief, Membertou.

Ritual and ceremonial dramas of First Peoples like the Mi'kmaq, various paratheatrical activities among early Viking and European explorers, and documented but unpublished performances by sixteenth-century Spaniards in Florida and New Mexico all jostle for the designation of "first North American play." One of the primary candidates for the honour has to be *Le Théâtre de Neptune en la Nouvelle-France*, written by lawyer, historian, and poet Marc Lescarbot in that tiny, short-lived French colony of Port Royal—the future Lower Granville, Nova Scotia—where it was performed on 14 November 1606 "on the waves," according to Lescarbot, and along the shore of what today is called the Annapolis Basin. Unlike its competitors, the play was published and has survived as a script and literary artifact as well as a carefully documented performance. A rich store of theatrical, historical, and political detail, *The Theatre of Neptune in New France* vividly illustrates *homo ludens*, the human imperative to play, at a crossroads of art and ideology. It provides an unparalleled glimpse into the lost world of early seventeenth-century North America, co-existing as a dense archeological site of early modern theatre history, a window into colonial North American social history and ethnography, and a snapshot of European strategies for imperial conquest.

As a living colonial artifact in a postcolonial age, the play still has the power to engage—and enrage. In response to a Nova Scotia theatre company's plans to celebrate the historical milestone of *Neptune*'s four hundredth anniversary by re-enacting it on site on that date, Montreal's Optative Theatrical Laboratories developed a project called *Sinking Neptune* to counter such celebrations. Presenting it as a work-in-progress, first at the Anarchist Theatre Festival and then at the inFRINGEment Festival in Montreal during the spring of 2006, Optative characterized *The Theatre of Neptune* as "an extremely racist play ... designed to subjugate First Nations through the appropriation of their identities, collective voices and lands." Through "masquerade and role appropriation, the play attempts to re-frame First Nation cultures into an exploitative Euro-centric social reality, and re-cast aboriginal peoples as subordinates" (King 5–7). For two years leading up to the anniversary, the company invited "political activists, theatre educators, culture-jammers" and others to help create a subversive, deconstructive counter-performance, "building a critical mass of cultural resistance to the play and re-enactment" (54). As we go to press in September of 2006, the *Sinking Neptune* project remains on track. But ironically, the re-enactment it was to confront in November has had to be cancelled for lack of Canada Council funding. What a quintessentially Canadian scenario. In any event these controversies indicate that after four hundred years *The Theatre of Neptune* remains a living, breathing dramatic enterprise, not just a theatrical museum piece. (See figs. 2 & 3.)

⟡

The Theatre of Neptune in New France was by no means the earliest Euro-American theatrical event. *The Cambridge History of American Theatre* lists four performances on its North American timeline preceding Lescarbot's play (Wilmeth and Bigsby 22–23). Spanish *comedias* were played in Florida in 1567 and Cuba in 1590. In 1598, just north of the Rio Grande in present-day New Mexico, Spanish soldiers performed an original comedy written by one of their officers in celebration of their conquests—"the first documented play written in the New World," though neither the script nor its title has survived (Davis 217). As well, various paratheatrical activities—*ludi*, or diversions, including musical ceremonies—may have taken place as early as 1000 A.D. among the Vikings who settled in Newfoundland, and on board

Fig. 2. Charles W. Jefferys's drawing for *The Theatre of Neptune in New France*, published in his popular *Picture Gallery of Canadian History* (1942). This has become the standard scenario by which to imagine the staging of the play. Courtesy of Library and Archives Canada (C-106968).

Fig. 3. Optative Theatrical Laboratories' poster for their *Sinking Neptune* project plays on Jefferys's popular drawing. Courtesy of Donovan King.

the ships that took Jacques Cartier to Hochelaga (Montreal) in 1535 and
Martin Frobisher farther north in 1576 (Gardner 1982, 7, 114–32). David
Gardner argues that the first Canadian theatrical performance may have
occurred as a "kind of folkloric prototheatre" in the form of mumming
during Sir Humphrey Gilbert's voyage to Newfoundland, either on board
his ship *Delight* or on shore in St. John's harbour in August 1583, where
Gilbert "took possession of Newfoundland" for the English queen in a
formal ceremony. Gardner makes his case based on first-hand reports that
musicians accompanied the expedition along with such "toyes as Morris
dancers, Hobby Horsse, and Maylike conceits to delight the Savage people"
(Gardner 1983, 227).

But *The Theatre of Neptune* is certainly the first theatrical script to have
been written and produced in what would become Canada. Its 1609
publication also represents a literary landmark of early Americana, marking
the beginning of American literature in the Harris Collection of American
Poetry and Plays in Brown University's John Hay Library ("Early American
Literature"). We have an account of the production from the playwright
himself; a brief eye-witness confirmation of Lescarbot's *gaillardise*
(translated as "jollity" or "jovial spectacle") by Samuel de Champlain,
published in Champlain's 1613 *Voyages* (see fig. 4); and an extant script with

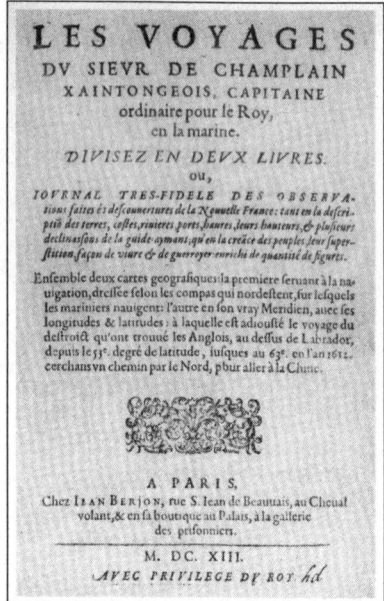

Fig. 4. Title page of Champlain's *Voyages*.
Published in Paris in 1613, it included
Champlain's version of many of the same
people and events Lescarbot described in his
1609 *Histoire de la Nouvelle-France*.

detailed production commentary (though how accurate it may be, we cannot know) preserved by Lescarbot in an appendix to his popular *Histoire de la Nouvelle-France*, published in Paris in 1609 and reprinted four times by 1618. Written by a member of the community and performed on site by soldiers, sailors, and artisans of the garrison, the play tells us a good deal about the life of that early North American settlement and the intrinsic importance of theatre to its survival.

This first published play written and performed in North America represents, in Richard Schechner's terms, a movement back and forth across the continuum of ritual and theatre, a braiding of entertainment and efficacy (performance enacted to effect transformations) no less organic than that of the dramatic ceremonials created and performed by the land's original inhabitants. *The Theatre of Neptune* was performance intended to divert and entertain as well as to create, reinforce, and ensure the present and future well-being of its participants: performance that, in Schechner's words, "makes happen what it celebrates" (128). "[W]hen efficacy and entertainment are both present in equal degrees—theater flourishes," he argues, citing as an example the Elizabethan era coterminous with Lescarbot's work (134). Although *The Theatre of Neptune* was a one-time-only event, it retains a theatrical potency that can be fully understood only by looking at the historical moment of the play and the material conditions of its performance in its original contexts.

⟐

In November 1606, Port Royal was the only European settlement in the Americas north of Florida. The French had continued fishing off Newfoundland and trading for furs along the St. Lawrence River after Jacques Cartier and the Sieur de Roberval abandoned their colony at Québec in 1543. But not until after 1598, when the Edict of Nantes and the Treaty of Vervins ended long-standing religious and civil conflicts and the war between France and Spain, did France try again to put down roots in its new world territories. In 1604 Pierre du Gua, Sieur de Monts received a charter from King Henri IV to explore and colonize the lands of La Cadie from latitude 40° to 46° (stretching from approximately present-day Philadelphia north to Prince Edward Island), and to convert the natives therein, in exchange for a monopoly of the fur trade. Accompanied by Champlain, who had helped map the St. Lawrence region the previous year, the 1604 expedition established its base camp on a small island that de Monts christened *Ile Sainte-Croix*. It sat along the north shore of *la Baie*

Française (the Bay of Fundy), where the future state of Maine would meet the future province of New Brunswick. After a terrible winter during which fifty-five of the seventy-nine male colonists contracted scurvy, thirty-five of them dying of it (Champlain 304), de Monts moved the settlement to a more sheltered spot across the bay in 1605, on the southern shore of a peninsula near the mouth of what is now the Annapolis River in Nova Scotia. He named the harbour *Port-Royal* and constructed a small fort, the *Habitation*. De Monts then returned to France. (See fig. 5.)

In the spring of 1606 Jean de Biencourt, Sieur de Poutrincourt, who had accompanied de Monts on the first voyage, set sail again from France on the frigate *Jonas* to take charge of the Port Royal colony which de Monts had ceded to him. On board was another Renaissance man, the Parisian humanist lawyer Marc Lescarbot, called by his first American biographer "the French Hakluyt" (see Biggar). In his *History of New France* Lescarbot explained that he was desirous "to explore the district with my own eyes" and, somewhat mysteriously, "to flee an evil world" (II:286–87). Born sometime around 1570 in Vervins, northeast of Paris, where the historic treaty would be signed, Lescarbot received a rich classical education while

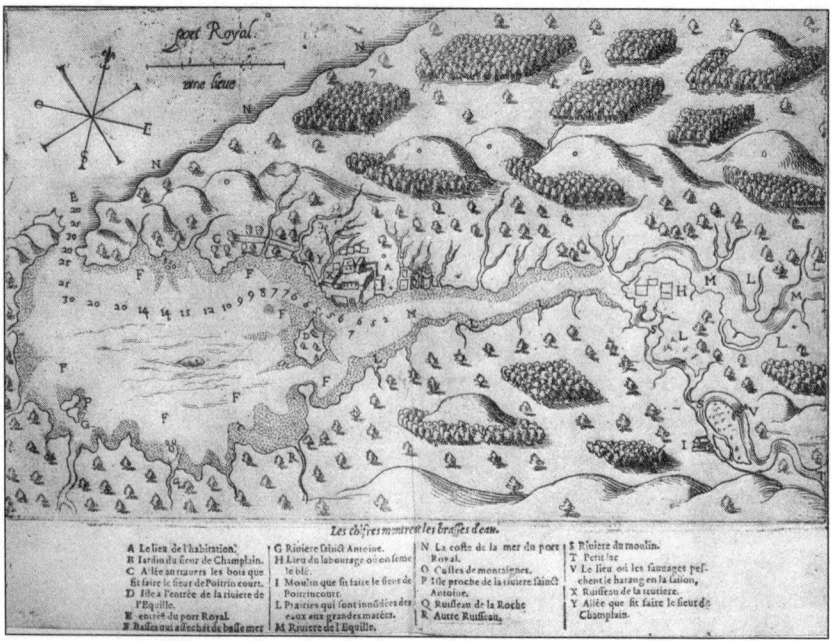

Fig. 5. Champlain's map of Port Royal with the *Habitation* at the centre, published in his 1613 *Voyages*.

studying law in Paris and Toulouse. Called to the bar in 1599, he had distinguished himself with Latin speeches thanking the Florentine Cardinal de Medici for his success in brokering the treaty negotiations between France and Spain at Vervins, and with his translations of two Latin ecclesiastical texts (Thierry 53–54, 74, 84). Soured by an "injustice" done to him in court by certain judges in favour of a *"personage d'eminente qualité,"* possibly a senior bishop—or perhaps just generally disgusted with what he considered a corrupted civilization—Lescarbot accepted an invitation from Poutrincourt, for whom he had done some legal work, to accompany him to the new world in 1606 (Thierry 2001, 100; Emont 58–62; see also Baudry). He remained there for a little more than a year, returning to the evil old world in the fall of 1607 and recounting his experiences in *The History of New France*. In it he also detailed the exploratory voyages of Verrazano, Cartier, Poutrincourt, and others; told the history of the St. Croix Island and Port Royal settlements; described at length the aboriginal inhabitants of that northerly environment; and appended a collection of poems, *Les Muses de la Nouvelle-France*, which included the versified *Théâtre de Neptune*, the only play he ever wrote. (See fig. 6.)

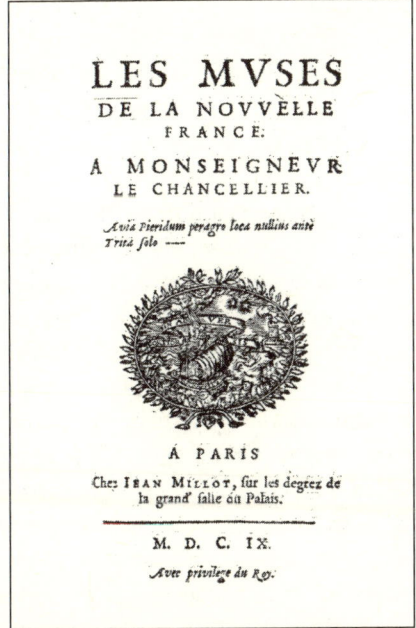

Fig. 6. Title page of Lescarbot's *Les Muses de la Nouvelle-France*.

Lescarbot departed Port Royal for France in 1607, along with all his compatriots, only because the settlement was abandoned when de Monts's fur trade monopoly was suddenly terminated by Henri IV. Champlain would return to New France the following year and re-establish, this time permanently, the settlement of Québec. Meanwhile, left in the care of the Mi'kmaq chief Membertou, the Port Royal *Habitation* was briefly re-occupied by Poutrincourt in 1610 and finally destroyed in 1613 by a British expedition from Virginia. Over the next century the area passed back and forth between the French and English in a series of military campaigns and political manoeuvres, with both the Mi'kmaq and French Acadian inhabitants increasingly marginalized, until the English took permanent control in 1710 and gave the garrison and community its present designation, Annapolis Royal. After five printings of his popular *Histoire* and a further career as lawyer, poet, historian, and sometime diplomat, Lescarbot died in France in 1641.

The occasion for the play was the return of Poutrincourt and Champlain from a voyage they had taken down the coast as far south as modern-day Martha's Vineyard, Massachusetts, in the late summer and fall of 1606. They had sailed in search of yet another site for a colony with "a suitable harbour in a good climate," Poutrincourt having deemed the health benefits of Port Royal's locale and weather no better than those of St. Croix Island (*History* II:318). The winter of 1605–06, although milder than their first, had still left twelve of the forty-five Port Royal colonists dead of scurvy (Champlain 375–76). Poutrincourt put Lescarbot in charge of Port Royal while he was gone, enjoining him "to keep an eye on the place, and to keep the peace among those who remained" (*History* II:319).

Lescarbot tackled his new responsibilities with relish. Unlike Poutrincourt, he saw Port Royal as a kind of paradise, a "spot more pleasant than any other in the world." He lavished praise on its hills, meadows, and streams, its abundant river, and its beautiful harbour with "two most fair and goodly islands" (II:234). A recent biographer describes Lescarbot as a new Adam in a new Eden (Thierry 2001, 118). The citified lawyer expressed his delight "in digging and tilling my gardens, fencing them in against the gluttony of the swine, making terraces, preparing straight alleys, building store-houses, sowing wheat, rye, barley, oats, beans, peas, garden plants, and watering them, so great a desire had I to know the soil by personal experience" (*History* II:266). In addition to its agricultural activities Lescarbot oversaw the settlement's other business, including hunting, gathering shellfish, digging drainage ditches around the *Habitation*, making charcoal for baking, and bartering bread for fish and game with the local Mi'kmaq people, whom the

French called Souriquois (II:319–20). The settlement's priest having died earlier that year, Lescarbot even preached on Sundays. "Nor was my labour without fruit," he mildly boasts, "many bearing me witness that never had they heard such good exposition of Divine things" (II:267).

Meanwhile, the *History* retrospectively describes the "many perils" of Poutrincourt and his crew's exploratory voyage as reported to Lescarbot and recounted first-hand by Champlain in his *Voyages*. Their misadventures among the warlike Armouchiquois as they sailed along the coast of the future Maine, Rhode Island, and Massachusetts left significant French and Native fatalities in their wake (see fig. 7). Unable to locate a site offering a milder climate, functional harbour, and more hospitable Natives, they set sail for the return voyage to Port Royal only to find themselves in heavy weather with a broken rudder. Just two days before their arrival they had an accident which they feared might sink their eighteen-ton *barque*. Even "at the

Fig. 7. Champlain's graphic illustration of the battles between Poutrincourt's men and the local Nauset people at Port Fortuné—"Misfortune harbor, so named by us on account of the misfortune which happened to us there" (Champlain 423)—on 14–16 October 1606. The site is present-day Stage Harbour, near Cape Cod, Massachusetts.

entrance to Port Royal," Champlain reports, "we were almost lost upon a point" (438). So it must have been as great a relief for the Poutrincourt expedition finally to reach safe harbour as it was for those left behind in the *Habitation* to see its return. (See fig. 8.)

With the colony's leader gone ten weeks, no sign of help from France, and winter fast approaching, the remaining inhabitants of Port Royal had grown seriously anxious and even mutinous, Lescarbot suggests. He writes of the joy and thanksgiving with which they greeted Poutrincourt's safe deliverance, and the celebratory performance they contrived to mark it:

> After many perils, which I shall not compare to those of Ulysses or of Aeneas, lest I stain our holy voyages amid such impurity, M. de Poutrincourt reached Port Royal on November 14th, where we received him joyously and with a ceremony (*une solennité*) absolutely new on that side of the ocean. For about the time we were expecting his return, whereof we had great desire, the more so that if evil had come upon him

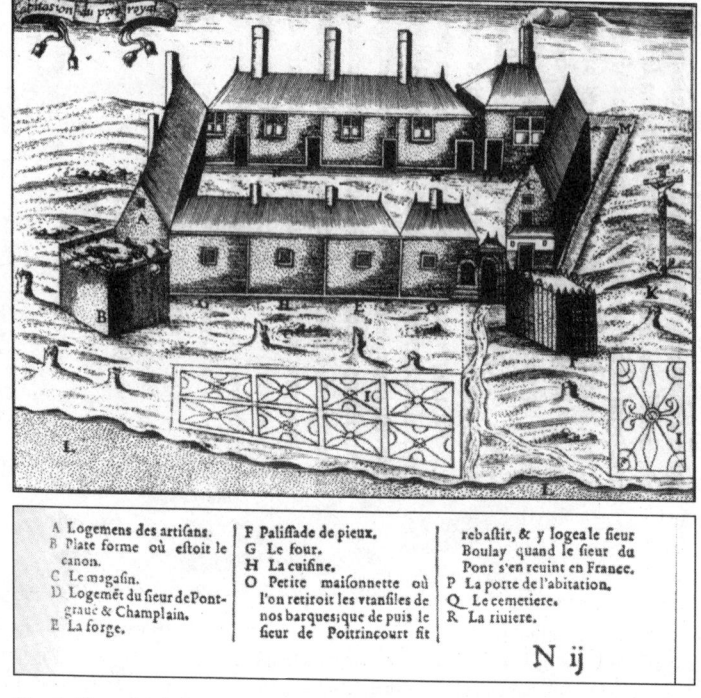

A Logemens des artiſans.	F Paliſſade de pieux.	rebaſtir, & y logea le ſieur
B Plate forme où eſtoit le canon.	G Le four.	Boulay quand le ſieur du
C Le magaſin.	H La cuiſine.	Pont s'en reuint en France.
D Logemết du ſieur dePont-grauc & Champlain.	O Petite maiſonnette où l'on retiroit les vtanſiles de	P La porte de l'abitation.
E La forge.	nos barquesique de puis le ſieur de Poittrincourt fit	Q Le cemetiere.
		R La riuiere.

N ij

Fig. 8. Champlain's drawing of the Port Royal *Habitation*, from his 1613 *Voyages*.

we had been in danger of a mutiny (*de la confusion*), I bethought me to go out to meet him with some jovial spectacle (*quelque gaillardise*), and so we did. And since it was written in French rhymes, made hastily, I have placed it among the *Muses of New France*, under the title of "Neptune's Theatre," to which I refer the reader. (II:340–41, 566–67)

After the "public rejoicing" that greeted the expedition's return, Lescarbot recalls how Poutrincourt, at Champlain's suggestion, established the Order of Good Cheer (*L'Ordre de Bon Temps*) to ensure that the colonists had a healthy, balanced diet. Each day a different man was appointed chief steward and made responsible for supplementing the usual fare with some special fish, meat, or fowl. These meals were often attended by "the Sagamos Membertou, and other chiefs" of the Souriquois, who "sat at table, eating and drinking like ourselves. And we were glad to see them, while, on the contrary, their absence saddened us.... " (II:344). Consciously using the honorific Mi'kmaq word for chief (*Sagamos*), Lescarbot claims that the French shared a mutual admiration with the Native people, *les Sauvages*—a term encompassing a range of meanings not at all fully reflected by the English word *savages* (Miller 31–32): "[A]nd hereby one may know that we were not, as it were, marooned on an island ... for this tribe loves the French, and would at need take up arms, one and all, to aid them" (II:344). Whatever the truth value of this claim, and despite the problematics of Lescarbot's Franco-Christian imperialism and Noble Savage romanticism, he remains consistent throughout the *History* in praising these people "of noble and generous heart" and "great liberality" (II:352). The local inhabitants comprised for Lescarbot one of the primary elements of his community's complex ecology of survival, which included the physical environment itself, the real and symbolic power of Poutrincourt, and the food and drink, both real and symbolic, at the dinner table and in *The Theatre of Neptune*.

Scholars have described *The Theatre of Neptune in New France* as a pageant, a triumphal entry (*entrée*), a *réception*, or a masque—all of which are sometimes subsumed under the term *fête*, or court festival. In his book on the theatre of early French Canada, Leonard E. Doucette explains that the play falls within the European tradition of "public masques and triumphal entries, the nautical extravaganzas and allegorical galas so integral to French (and English) courtly life since the Renaissance. The triumphal entries in particular, where the king's household received the corresponding cortege coming out from the town through which he wished to pass ... seem to have influenced Lescarbot's work" (7). In a typical *réception* or *entrée royale*,

> [t]he personage was normally welcomed by the more important residents and escorted to his destination where he was offered a feast. In the case of the ruler or his representative, he was also offered reassurances of their loyalty by representatives of the various orders of inhabitants. The entry was the visible sign of a contract between ruler and subject town, the ruler assuring the prosperity and protection of the town by his power; the town, in return, offering its loyalty and all its resources in exchange.... The ordered form of the entry expressed symbolically the relationship between the entering dignitary and the townspeople, as well as providing an opportunity for communal rejoicing and solidarity. (Fournier 3)

Glen Nichols has identified eight other *réceptions* performed in French Canada between 1648 and 1810 to receive and honour dignitaries ranging from the headmaster of a school to the governor of Québec. Like *The Theatre of Neptune*, all were produced expressly for one particular event and all directly address by name at least one individual present in the audience for the performance (Nichols 72). In Lescarbot's pageant the god Neptune and his Tritons along with the Indians and the "companion of jolly disposition" from the colony offer their praise and allegiance, their loyalty and foodstuffs directly to Poutrincourt, the King's representative and living symbol of French power, on the occasion of his safe return. Through the symbolism of performance, the play dramatically reinforces the contract between ruler and ruled that promises the subjects' survival and prosperity in return for their fealty.

Lescarbot's nautical spectacle cites a full century's development of the European arts of courtly celebration. As Roy Strong argues, "A tremendous revolution had taken place in which, under the impact of Renaissance humanism, the [medieval] art of festival was harnessed to the emergent modern state as an instrument of rule.... [I]ts fundamental objective was power conceived as art.... In the court festival, the Renaissance belief in man's ability to control his own destiny and harness the natural resources of the universe find their most extreme assertion" (1984, 19, 40). Drawing on classical mythology and the sometimes arcane language of neo-Platonic emblems and devices, these celebrations affirmed visually and verbally the magnificence of Renaissance rulers in their ability to effect spectacular transformations in both the natural and human realms, enabling a harmony "which centred on political power being a reflection of a geocentric universe" (40).

The learned Lescarbot would have been familiar with these spectacles not only through first-hand experience but via the print and visual forms, including elaborate published accounts with engravings, by which most major events of this kind were recorded. For archival and political purposes the court festivals and royal entries were preserved in manuscripts, statues and triumphal arches, and printed festival books: "[T]he whole effort of *memoria* engaged in by every court during this period ... [was] driven by the desire to mitigate the transience of an event by pinning it down for posterity, by the necessity to manufacture the official story of that court in order to create *fama, Ruhm, gloire* and in this way to outwit mortality" (Watanabe-O'Kelly 19–20). Lescarbot pursued this same impulse in transcribing and publishing *The Theatre of Neptune*, his detailed, after-the-fact recording of the *fête* he staged upon the waves and shore of Port Royal.

In France Lescarbot had access to a substantial record of recent triumphal entries involving nautical motifs derived from the revival of the imperial Roman *naumachia*, or mock sea battles, and other water festivals employing the sea god, his nymphs, and tritons. More than one publication documented the spectacular entry of Henri II into Rouen in 1550 after his defeat of the English at Boulogne. As the king and his retinue crossed the bridge over the Seine, Neptune and other marine creatures appeared: "The king of the seas saluted Henri, offering him dominion over the waves; and as soon as the King of France had accepted Neptune's trident, the three sea creatures leapt into the river, there performing marvelous acrobatics amid the crowd of marine life which had surfaced to greet the French monarch" (McGowan 222). Surrounded by dolphins, whales, and triton-musicians, his chariot drawn by sea-horses and followed by swimming nymphs and sirens, Neptune assured the French king of favourable winds, calm seas, and the support of the gods if Henri were to sail off to conquer England (229). (See fig. 9.)

A *fête* celebrating Charles IX at Fontainebleau in 1564 featured Neptune in a chariot drawn by sea-horses on a canal (Strong 1984, 104), a configuration repeated much more elaborately the following year at Bayonne:

> [N]otables of both [the French and Spanish] courts boarded a magnificent boat in the shape of a castle and sailed through various canals to an island in the river, witnessing spectacles along the way. The first tableau was a mock whale hunt, which lasted half an hour; then the spectators saw six tritons, dressed in cloth of gold, playing trumpets on the back of a huge sea turtle. Next came Neptune in a great chariot pulled by sea horses, followed by Arion on a dolphin's back and three sirens who sang songs celebrating Charles IX's meeting with his sister, Elisabeth de Valois, the

Fig. 9. Illumination from *L'Entreé de Henri II à Rouen le 1er Octobre 1550*. Courtesy of Collections de la Bibliotèque municipale de Rouen. Photographies Thierry Ascencio-Parvy.

Note Neptune and his sea creatures on the right. On the left and at centre-foreground are some of the fifty Native people, brought to France from its Brazilian colony, who participated, naked, in the royal welcome (McGowan 218–19).

queen of Spain. After this they landed on the island, where shepherds and shepherdesses served a banquet, which was followed by a ballet danced by nine nymphs.... (Denison 18; see also Strong 1984, 105–09) (See fig. 10.)

For a royal wedding in Paris in 1572, Charles IX himself played the role of Neptune (Strong 1984, 112). Another wedding celebration, this one under the reign of Henri III in 1581, produced a river *fête* with a triumphal chariot "drawn by twenty-four little ships disguised as sea-horses, tritons, whales, sirens, tortoises, dolphins and other marine monsters, in which were concealed musicians and singers" (118–19), as well as one of the most celebrated spectacles of the age: Catherine de Medici's *Balet Comique de la Royne*, often considered "'the first genuine ballet de cour' and an important step in the development of opera" (MacClintock 9). It featured the entrance of Queen Louise and her ladies dressed as naiads, in a pageant car drawn by sea-horses, escorted by tritons and sirens (Strong 1984, 120–22). (See figs. 11 & 12.)

Fig. 10. *The Water Festival at Bayonne, June 24, 1565,* by Antoine Caron. Neptune and his chariot and the triton-musicians on turtleback are in the left background. The Pierpont Morgan Library, New York, purchased as a gift of The Fellows 1955.7. Photograph courtesy of the Pierpont Morgan Library, New York.

Fig. 11. Engraving of triton-musicians from *Le Balet Comique de la Royne*, performed in 1581 and published in 1582. Courtesy of the Rare Book & Manuscript Library, University of Illinois.

Fig. 12. Sirens from *Le Balet Comique de la Royne*. Courtesy of the Rare Book & Manuscript Library, University of Illinois.

This represents only a small sampling of the French festivities that utilized the same mythological machinery at home that Lescarbot would employ abroad. Nautical masques, mock sea battles, and thespian Neptunes acknowledging their fealty and subordination to worldly princes and those princes' representatives were commonplace in France and widespread across the rest of Europe. In England in 1591, the Earl of Hertford welcomed Queen Elizabeth to his estate with a pageant staged on a large pond dug and filled especially for the occasion, a mock battle between the gods of the wood and the sea, the latter led by Neptune, Oceanus, their tritons, and marine retinue (Bergeron 57–60). Two spectacularly illustrated volumes commemorating royal entries into Antwerp in the 1590s, published with nautical themes and Latin texts in 1595 and 1602 in that nearby city, would likely have been available to Lescarbot (*Ceremonial Entry*). (See fig. 13.)

French writers, artists, and other mythmakers in the last decade of the old century and the first decade of the new saw a special providence in the ascension of Henri de Navarre to the throne in 1589 as Henri IV, the first of the Bourbon kings. Equally renowned for his political judgment and his warrior skills, a Huguenot convert to Catholicism whose Edict of Nantes

Fig. 13. Pieter van der Borcht's engraving of Neptune riding a whale, from the Archduke of Austria's entry into Antwerp, 1594, published 1595. Courtesy of the Museum Plantin-Moretus, Antwerp. Photography by Peter Maes.

guaranteed religious rights to Protestants, and who, it seemed, might re-unite Christian Europe—his marriage to Maria de Medici in 1600 promising further strategic alliances—Henri was celebrated as the second coming of Charlemagne, a "Gallic Hercules" under whose reign a new golden age of imperial power, universal peace, and neo-classical culture could emerge: "In all the most impressive humanistic output of the time we find the same themes of praise [for Henri] auguring a new civilized way of life, new human relations, and a differently organized state under the protection of a sovereign armed with the sword of Justice" (Vivanti 192). (Modern biographies are not quite so flattering [see Buisseret], and in any case the dream ended with Henri's assassination in 1610.) The tributes Lescarbot's characters offer to Poutrincourt reflect this king's perceived virtues and glories, embodied at that time and place in Poutrincourt, his new world deputy. When Neptune encourages Poutrincourt's imperial ventures on behalf of Henri in Lescarbot's play, he is also echoing an episode in the king's spectacular 1595 entry into Lyons. At a certain point in the procession three Victories handed their crowns to Henri; the second one, extending him a naval crown, prophesied France's conquest of the Americas. You will pass victoriously through the pillars of Hercules, he told the king, receive Mars's sword and Neptune's trident, and under your reign the *fleur de lys* will fly triumphant again over Florida and all the Western isles (Vivanti 190).

A little over a decade later, as Lescarbot's company was welcoming the king's deputy in Port Royal, Shakespeare's company was preparing *King Lear* in London. In the opening court scene of Shakespeare's play, which premiered only six weeks after the performance of *The Theatre of Neptune*, we might hear faint echoes of Lescarbot's ritual theatre when Lear's daughters individually offer him their formal praise. But almost immediately Cordelia subverts the ceremony and challenges the royal power, introducing the conflict necessary to drive tragedy—conflict conspicuously absent from celebratory pageants like *Neptune*. Its power-flattering ritual formality resonates more fully with "the kind of action masques present ... [which] can take place only in a world purged of drama, of conflict" (Orgel 17). Such were the masques Ben Jonson and Inigo Jones jointly created for the contemporary Stuart court of England, beginning with *The Masque of Blackness*, contrived upon an artificial sea for presentation in Whitehall Palace before King James I and Queen Anne on Twelfth Night, 6 January 1605. The French *réception* closely mirrored the English and French courtly masques, those formal theatrical expressions of honorific praise utilizing music, allegorical poetry, and elaborate costumes and scenery in celebration of their royal audience. Although the ultra-civilized nautical masque may seem incongruous when re-imagined in and transposed to the real seas and relative wilderness of New France, its ability to conjure the wealth and majesty of the imperial power centre would have been precisely its point. As Jonas Barish has written of the Jonsonian masque, it "may be taken as a kind of mimetic magic on a sophisticated level, the attempt to secure social health and tranquility for the realm by miming it in front of its chief figure" (244).

Alan Filewod describes the court masque as "a spectacular artifact that harnessed complex systems of technological production, labour and artisan craft to display the power of the state that summoned it" (xii). In the face of potentially mutinous colonists, aboriginals who could quickly turn hostile—notwithstanding Lescarbot's claim of mutual respect—and the onset of what might very well have been another killing winter, Lescarbot's masque harnessed whatever theatrical technologies were available to him in that remote colonial outpost to invoke the state's civil, military, and spiritual powers embodied in the King's representative. Despite his disclaimer that he would not "stain our holy voyages" with the impurity of classical comparisons, Lescarbot immediately introduces the Roman god of the sea who personally offers support and protection for the French enterprise. Trumpets sound and cannons thunder in a spectacular display of military pomp and power, concluding with the jolly companion's announcement of the actual feast that would follow. This "new world masque" encoded "cultural hegemony through the assertion of dominant myth," promising "not just esthetic pleasure but actual survival" (Bowers 50).

The pragmatics of the masque can be traced back, through mumming and *ludi*, to its origins in ritual performances in aid of the communal food supply (see Welsford, ch. 1–2). The efficacy of *The Theatre of Neptune* for the Port Royal colonists had multiple dimensions: "as a cathartic entertainment relieving the settlers of Port Royal from the anxiety caused by the prolonged absence of their leader; as a political statement expressing the loyalty of the new world colony to their ruler and representative of the King of France, Henri IV; and as an act of sympathetic magic intending to subdue the hostile natural environment and native peoples to the rule of French imperial civilization" (Wagner 7).

The subdued natural environment immediately appears in a conventional Renaissance expression of the familiar notion that God is on our side. Neptune himself guarantees the cooperation of the sea, praising Poutrincourt for his "many brilliant deeds ... in the French war." (Ironically, Poutrincourt had originally distinguished himself fighting *against* Henri in the early

1590s, but came over to his side after the king's conversion and became one of his most valued allies.) Neptune pledges Poutrincourt his perpetual allegiance and assistance for the French imperial project in the new world, vowing never to rest "Until I see my waves in this area / Pant under the weight of ten thousand [French] ships." (I cite the Bensons' translation throughout this introduction.) If further reassurance were necessary, the Third Triton adds that Neptune "will always support you and yours / Against all human power." (See fig. 14.)

The homage of the Indians, *les Sauvages*, representative of both human power and the natural world, offers further evidence that Nature has been subdued to Culture, savagery to civilization. In perfect French they vow to Poutrincourt to "devote ourselves to you / And to your descendants," not merely accepting their colonial subservience but embracing it. (In the *History* Lescarbot claims that Membertou and his Souriquois people wept at the departure of the French in 1607, comforted only by the promise "that next year we should send households and families to dwell permanently in their land, and to teach them trades in order to help them to live like us" [II:364]. Membertou himself was baptized a Catholic in 1610.) Finally, the companion invokes a Rabelaisian indulgence, addressing a fictitious array of "grillers, waiters, cooks, / ... bakers ... tavern keepers," as though all the culinary riches of Paris were awaiting them rather than another bleak winter of potential malnutrition. This is performance not only as sympathetic magic but as sheer wish-fulfillment fantasy. This conclusion also effects the breaching of the barrier between spectators and actors that Stephen Orgel argues was an essential component of the court masque, "so that in effect the viewer became part of the spectacle." Whereas in the Jonsonian masque this transformation generally occurred in the revels—the dance between masquers and audience members (Orgel 6–7)—in Lescarbot's pageant the feast that followed, *sans* dance, represented this apotheosis of communal identification.

As for what Schechner calls the entertainment braid, Filewod argues on the basis of its logistical situation that the performance of *The Theatre of Neptune* could have been only "a roughly sketched quotation of Lescarbot's memories of the ... ornate spectacles produced by sophisticated mechanics" in the masques and royal entries he had seen in France (xii). Yet, if we can believe his own stage directions, Lescarbot managed to deploy a wide array of impressive effects, literal and theatrical, in the site-specific staging of his spectacle for his two audiences: Poutrincourt out there "on the waves" and the French and Native people on the shore. Neptune—costumed, wigged,

Fig. 14. Neptune's chariot, from the entry of Albrecht and Isabella into Antwerp, 1599. Engraving by Pieter van der Borcht, published in 1602. This commemorated a special kind of ceremonial entry, a *joyeuse entrée* or *Blijde Inkomst*, the first time the ruler or his/her governor entered one of the main towns of the country (Mielke VII).

The kind of power mythologically (and somewhat baroquely) invoked in this image suggests what Lescarbot was aiming for. Courtesy of the Museum Plantin-Moretus, Antwerp. Photography by Peter Maes.

and bearded—holds a prop trident and rides in a decorated set piece that also had to be a functional boat: a sea-going "chariot" drawn by the six Tritons rowing up to six additional vessels, probably canoes. (Such chariots and tritons on *artificial* seas were common elements of the ornate spectacles and sophisticated mechanics of many contemporary court masques, including *The Masque of Blackness*, in which the royal masquers rode the theatrical waves in "a great concave shell like mother of pearl," while their attendants were borne on the backs of "six huge sea-monsters.") Paddling out into the harbour to meet Poutrincourt's ship, or ship's boat (the shallop), as it approaches shore, Lescarbot's Tritons are cued by the sound effect of a trumpet. The Indians—surely Frenchmen in Native costume, not the Mi'kmaq themselves as has sometimes been speculated—each offer a gift which is, like Poutrincourt's sword, at once both a prop and the real thing: a quarter of elk or moose, beaver skins, bracelets. After the speeches in which Lescarbot shows off his literary skills—flourishing classical rhetoric and allusion, varied verse forms and dialects, and notes of comic relief—Neptune's troupe sings a song. More trumpets and the grand military spectacle of a quarter-hour's worth of cannon fire follow. The play ends with the beaching of the smaller boats as Poutrincourt comes ashore to a ritual joke ("Before drinking, let each one sneeze loudly") and a trilingual toast by the jolly companion with what is no doubt real wine.

Thematically, *The Theatre of Neptune* embodies an early example of what Margaret Atwood, in 1972, would famously declare to be Canada's prototypical literary concern: survival. In his *History*, immediately after writing about the performance of *The Theatre of Neptune*, Lescarbot provides an account of the establishment of the Order of Good Cheer, the primary means by which the colonists were to avoid the scourge of scurvy which had killed so many of their fellows over the previous two winters. As Schechner has said of certain kinds of ritual celebrations, "what starts as theater ends as Communion" (116). Food preparation and dining also became ritual performances that winter, no less efficacious than the nautical *réception* that celebrated the successful transition of the colony from leaderless, near-mutinous contingency to god-blessed safety and stability.

The play also provides a prototype for the theatrical presentation of Native peoples in a great many subsequent North American plays. François Moureau suggests that Lescarbot modeled his aboriginal characters in *Le Théâtre de Neptune* on already theatricalized stock characters, or "masks," purportedly Native American, that he had seen performing in *ballets de cour* in France before he set sail for Port Royal—although most of the examples

Moureau offers date from after 1606 (44). In the four hundred years since then, Euro-Canadian and -American playwrights have frequently written aboriginal characters into their theatrical portraits of the land and its history, usually either demonizing or romanticizing them. But rarely, until Native North American dramatists themselves began creating more realistic theatrical self-portraiture in the 1980s, have they been presented in any form but that of the Imaginary Indian, "the invention of the European" (Francis 4), a notion never more clear than in Lescarbot's noble savages who spout Parisian verse and cheerlead their own surrender to imperial French rule.

Yet despite what some call the "racial impersonation and colonial masquerade" (Filewod xv) of a play "designed to subjugate First Nations through the appropriation of their identities, collective voice, and lands" (King 5–6), Lescarbot rarely patronizes the Native characters of his dramatic poetry or history, and frequently gives them substantial dignity. He is certainly guilty of the cultural imperialism of which Optative's Donovan King accuses him in the *Sinking Neptune* project. Lescarbot undoubtedly also employs in the play, vis à vis his aboriginal characters and audience, the cultural strategies that Bruce McConachie, following Antonio Gramsci and Kenneth Burke, calls *the hegemonic we*, "whereby any social group persuades itself and attempts to persuade others that its own values and patterns of symbolic action are natural and right" (46, 44). And could it be otherwise that Lescarbot's aboriginals would be somewhat distorted by the imaginary and symbolic qualities his European perspective would attach to them—in Philip J. Deloria's particularly apropos phrase, "the visible products of the sea of ideology in which humans swim" (20).

Still, in the context of early seventeenth-century imperial European attitudes, Lescarbot's seems genuinely civil, or at least less toxic than most. I've already noted how, in the *History*, he consistently praises Souriquois manners and mores despite—and at times because of—their "heathen" ways. He devotes his entire Sixth Book, an extraordinary exercise in comparative ethnography, to "the Manners, Customs, and Fashions of Life of the Western Indians of New France" (III:xii). He celebrates Souriquois mothers for the great love they bear their children. They suckle their infants themselves, he notes, rather than giving them over to nursemaids as European women do, and they refuse to allow the French to take any of the children back to Europe: "Thus I consider that they are wronged in being called barbarous, seeing that the ancient Romans were far more barbarous, who oftentimes sold their children to obtain wherewith to live" (III:86–87). He admires Souriquois courtship and marital customs, and the chastity of the women, using biblical and classical references to underline their comparative virtues (III:161–65). He praises the Souriquois for their "ancient golden age" communal values, "the most perfect and most worthy life of man"; and for their hospitality, "a virtue which apparently endures only among the nobility and gentry" of contemporary Europe, "for among other classes we see it sick unto death" (III:174). When it comes to trade, the local peoples "have nothing but frankness and liberality in their exchanging." They show fatherly piety ("the children are not so cursed as to despise their parents in old age ... the shame of many Christians") and "humanity and mercy towards their enemies' wives and little children" (III:214–15). "Our savages" he finds "more humane" than many European cultures in their funerary ceremonies (III:285). Though mildly criticizing the Native people for their ancient custom of interring valuables along with their dead, he ends the chapter, and his *History*, by pointing out that the Spaniards "and our own men ... void of all humanity" are the ones who engage in the genuinely savage practice of robbing Native graves (III:288).

Lescarbot also registers his respect for his Native hosts by incorporating (or appropriating, depending on one's perspective) indigenous vocabulary from the local language into *The Theatre of Neptune*. In the script he footnotes and translates *Sagamos*, for captain or chief; *adesquidés*, meaning friend; and *caracona*, or bread. These words signify the elements most important to the colony's survival: authority and order, solidarity and mutual assistance, and sustenance. In a stage direction he also glosses the Souriquois word *Matachiaz*, meaning trinkets and bracelets. Even if the Indian characters are imaginary, the dependency of European colonists on the Native inhabitants' cooperation, assistance, foodstuffs, and trade goods was entirely real, and would remain so throughout the seventeenth century and beyond (see Miller, ch. 2).

⁓

On account of its ephemeral nature (a single performance on a special occasion); or because the genre went out of style; or because the Port Royal settlement was abandoned; or because the French lost not just the political but the cultural wars; or because Lescarbot and his chronicles of New France were superseded by Champlain and his (for the "feud" between Lescarbot and Champlain, see Armstrong 284–89; Thierry 2004); likely for all these reasons, *Le Théâtre de Neptune en la Nouvelle-France* quickly disappeared from public memory, not to re-emerge for more than three centuries. Only in 1926 was its historical significance finally acknowledged when the Lieutenant Governor of Nova Scotia, on behalf of the Historical Association of Annapolis Royal, dedicated a plaque at the site of the Port Royal *Habitation* commemorating the first drama written and produced in Canada. In his October 1926 theatre column in *Canadian Forum* magazine, Fred Jacobs wrote, "Can you imagine our cousins across the line neglecting such a possession as we have done?... If it belonged to American history, every child in that country would probably be able to tell you about Lescarbot and to spout at least a verse or two from his play" (416).

In fact, the campaign to rebuild the *Habitation* as a national historic site was spearheaded by an American historical enthusiast, Harriette Taber Richardson of Cambridge, Massachusetts, who established the Associates of Port Royal in the United States to raise money for the reconstruction (see Schmeisser). Richardson also translated the play into English for the first time and read her translation at the 1926 commemoration. Parts of Lescarbot's *Histoire de la Nouvelle-France* had appeared in English as early as 1609 (see fig. 15), but a full English version, translated by W. L. Grant for

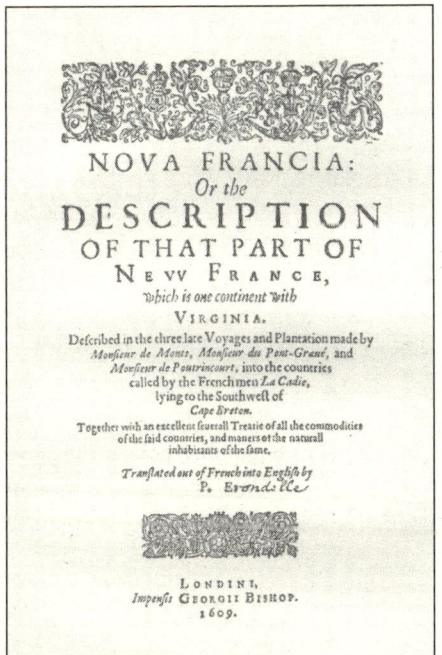

NOVA FRANCIA:
Or the
DESCRIPTION
OF THAT PART OF
NEVV FRANCE,
vvhich is one continent vvith
VIRGINIA.

Described in the three late Voyages and Plantation made by *Monsieur de Monts, Monsieur du Pont-Grané,* and *Monsieur de Poutrincourt,* into the countries called by the Frenchmen *La Cadie,* lying to the Southwest of *Cape Breton.*
Together with an excellent severall treatie of all the commodities of the said countries, and maners of the naturall inhabitants of the same.

Translated out of French into English by P. Erondelle.

LONDINI,
Impensis GEORGII BISHOP.
1609.

Fig. 15. Title page of *Nova Francia*, the abbreviated first English version of Lescarbot's *Histoire de la Nouvelle-France*, translated by Pierre Erondelle and published in London in 1609.

Fig. 16. Interior courtyard of the reconstructed Port Royal *Habitation*. Courtesy of *Wikipedia*. Photograph by Danielle Langlois.

the Champlain Society, had to wait until 1911; and both versions omitted the poetic appendix *Les Muses de la Nouvelle-France*, which included the long-forgotten *Theatre of Neptune*. Canadian scholar R. Keith Hicks published his own translation of the play in 1926 and Richardson's appeared in print the following year. A 350th anniversary re-enactment of the production was staged in 1956, with a cast of one hundred in full costume, on the waters of the Annapolis Basin before the *Habitation*, which had finally been restored in 1939 (Wagner 36–37) (see fig. 16). Illustrator Charles W. Jefferys, who had written about the restoration of Port Royal in the *Canadian Historical Review*, reconstructed what he imagined to be the original *mise en scène* of *The Theatre of Neptune* in a 1942 ink drawing for his popular and widely circulated *Picture Gallery of Canadian History* (see fig. 2). In 1963, Nova Scotia's new regional theatre centre was christened Neptune Theatre in honour of Lescarbot's play.

I present here the French script of *Le Théâtre de Neptune en la Nouvelle-France*, produced in 1606 and first published in 1609, along with the original English translation by Harriette Taber Richardson; the more recent translation of University of Guelph professors Eugene and Renate Benson, first published in the journal *Canadian Drama* in 1982; and Jonson and Jones's *The Masque of Blackness*, performed in 1605 and first published in 1608.

The Bensons' translation of *The Theatre of Neptune* is more literal and prosaic than the others. It makes no attempt to reproduce Lescarbot's Alexandrine metrics, rhythms, or rhyme schemes—Neptune's couplets, for instance—but "provide[s] a line-by-line translation that is accurate and functional," according to Eugene Benson, who offers this rationale:

> We offer this new translation not only because of the relative inaccessibility of the translation[s] made in the 1920s, but because they are often inaccurate. For example, R. K. Hicks ... turns the Fourth Indian's beautiful speech into pidgin English.... Richardson ... too often sacrifices accuracy in trying to preserve Lescarbot's Alexandrines. She translates "Jupiter eut le ciel, Pluton eut les Enfers" as "Jove rules the windy sky, Pluto the flaming heart." A simple translation best reveals the line's meaning: "Jupiter received the sky, Pluto the Underworld." (Benson 85)

Of the translators, Hicks certainly takes the most liberties. He changes the First Indian's *abab* rhyme scheme to couplets for no good reason. His Fourth Indian's pidgin speech is utterly bizarre and, to a contemporary ear, racist. The original reads:

SAGAMOS, pardonne moy
Si je viens en telle sorte,
Si me presentant à toy
Quelque present je n'apporte.

Hicks translates, "Red man bring no gift—no luck, bad hunting—Waw—beat woods all day—no moose—no deer—change business—give up hunting—Waw ... " and so on. The Bensons' translation is literal but somewhat prosaic:

SAGAMOS, pardon me
If I come in this manner,

> If, while presenting myself to you,
> I do not bring you any gifts.

Richardson is best here at capturing what Benson calls the Indian's "beautiful speech" as well as Lescarbot's poetry:

> Sagamos, pardon me,
> If before you, here, I stand,
> Present, in this company,
> With no present in my hand.

Richardson is not above utilizing a little pidgin English herself. The Fifth Triton's exotic Gascon dialect, though certainly a long way from the other characters' Parisian French, she renders in a metaphor difficult to comprehend:

> Listen, to what I want to say
> About dat high flown God Neptune!
> I caught de peacock—t'odder day
> Carryin' on lak one dragoon.

The Bensons' translation is clearer and less caricatured, but at the expense of the rhyme and much of the flavour of the original:

> Hear ye what I wish to say:
> That old fellow, Neptune,
> Bragged loudly the other day
> Admiring himself like a real ladies' man.

Hicks, again, is off the map:

> I go tell you what I tink.
> Old man Neptune naughty fellow,
> Dress himself in blue and yellow,
> Look himself in glass and wink.

On balance, the Bensons' literal translation probably works best for a contemporary reader whereas Richardson most effectively conveys a sense of Lescarbot the dramatic poet.

Ben Jonson and Inigo Jones's *The Masque of Blackness* is included here for comparative purposes. It provides an example of the allegorical spectacle of empire as it appeared in the English theatre, from the hands of a major playwright and the greatest stage designer of the age, almost exactly contemporary with Lescarbot's play. Both productions reference what Joseph Roach calls "the circum-Atlantic interculture" (5), memorializing "a persistent Atlantic occasion particularly subject to forgetting: encounters among white, red, and black peoples ... real or imagined, acting in one another's presence" (122). Although *The Tempest* has received the most critical attention as a theatrical vehicle of early modern colonial attitudes, the masques of empire were doing similar cultural work, sometimes in even more overt ways. Lescarbot and the team of Jonson and Jones employ the mythologies of Renaissance humanism along with the tools of contemporary stagecraft to reinforce the imperial fantasies popular in the courts of both France and England, and to naturalize the subordination of dark-skinned Others whose lands and bodies were increasingly claimed by those courts. The age of exploration was rapidly becoming the age of colonization across Europe. These spectacles, fascinating in their own theatrical right, can also be usefully understood as emissaries of the new imperial project.

A Note on the Texts

For the French text of *Le Théâtre de Neptune en la Nouvelle-France*, I have used volume 3 of the Champlain Society's 1914 edition of *The History of New France* by Marc Lescarbot (published in a limited edition of 520 copies; reprinted by Greenwood Press in 1968), which contains both the original French version of the *History* and W. L. Grant's English translation, as well as Lescarbot's appended collection of poems, *Les Muses de la Nouvelle-France*, untranslated. In the latter is found *Le Théâtre de Neptune* (473–79). Lescarbot's *Histoire de la Nouvelle-France* was first published in 1609. A second edition appeared in 1611 with another printing in 1612. An expanded third edition was published in 1617 and reprinted, virtually unaltered, in 1618. The Champlain Society text utilizes the 1618 printing, the final version of the book and play published during Lescarbot's lifetime. I follow Hannah Fournier's 1981 edition (*Canadian Drama* 7.1, 44–50) in regularizing the letters *v* and *u*, *i* and *j*. Otherwise I have retained the idiosyncracies of seventeenth-century French spelling and accents.

Harriette Taber Richardson's translation was published in a limited edition of 450 copies in Boston by Houghton Mifflin in 1927. Richardson also provides an intelligent, well-researched twelve-page introduction, a dozen illustrations, and the 1609 French text with notes on textual variants in the later editions. The *Dramatis Personae* with which she introduces the French text I have used to introduce her English version. Although she virtually dismisses the play as a "gay piece of courtly fun" (ix), she obviously invested a great deal of her time, energy, money, and personal reputation in successful efforts to resurrect the text, the *Habitation*, and the memory of "the gentlemen of Port Royal and … their polished courage" (xiv).

The translation by Eugene Benson and Renate Benson was first published in *Canadian Drama* 8.1 (1982) with a brief introduction by Eugene Benson and three of Lescarbot's maps. It was reprinted in *Colonial Quebec: French-Canadian Drama, 1606-1966*, volume 4 of Anton Wagner's *Canada's Lost Plays* series (35–43). The Bensons based their translation on the 1612 text as edited by Hannah Fournier in *Canadian Drama* 7.1.

My text of *The Masque of Blackness* is based on the standard edition in *Ben Jonson: The Complete Masques*, edited by Stephen Orgel (1969), which itself is based on the text of the masque in the eleven-volume standard edition of Ben Jonson's works, edited by C. H. Herford and Percy and Evelyn Simpson for the Clarendon Press. *The Masque of Blackness* appears on pages 169–80 of volume 7, published in 1941, with an introduction and notes in volume 10 (1950, 445–55). *The Masque of Blackness* was originally published in London in 1608 along with *The Masque of Beauty* in a Quarto. It was republished in the 1616 Folio of Jonson's plays and again in the 1640 Second Folio. Herford and the Simpsons base their text on the First Folio. I have taken some minor liberties with Orgel's edition, mostly in matters of spelling and punctuation where I think they make better sense, going back to Herford and the Simpsons in some cases, and in others following the choices of one or another modern editor, David Lindley (*Court Masques: Jacobean and Caroline Entertainments, 1605–1640*) or Richard Harp (*Ben Jonson's Plays and Masques*). Jonson himself provided extensive marginal notes to the masque, mostly in Latin and Greek. Herford and the Simpsons, Orgel, Lindley, and Harp all provide their own editorial and explanatory notes and definitions of some of Jonson's arcane or archaic terms. I have chosen not to reproduce Jonson's notes and to offer minimal notes of my own. I'm indebted to Professor Tony Dawson for his judicious help in deciding what to gloss and how to gloss it.

Le Théâtre de Neptune en la Nouvelle-France

❧

The Theatre of Neptune in New France

DE LA NOVVELLE. FRANCE. II
Neptune, si iamais tu as favorisé
Ceux qui dessus tes eaux leurs vies ont vsé;
Vray Neptune, fay nous chacun ou il desire
A bon port arriuer, afin que ton Empire
Soit par-deça coneu en maintes regions,
Et bien-tot frequenté de toutes nations.

LE THEATRE
DE NEPTVNE EN LA
NOVVELLE-FRANCE

Representé sur les flots du Port Royal le quator-
ziéme de Novembre mille six cens six, au retour
du Sieur de Poutrincourt du pais des Armou-
chiquois.

Neptune commence revetu d'vn voile de couleur
bleuë, & de brodequins, ayant la chevelure & la barbe
longues & chenuës, tenant son Trident en main,
assis sur son chariot paré de ses couleurs : ledit chariot trainé sur les ondes par six Tritons jusques à
l'abord de la chaloupe où s'estoit mis ledit Sieur de
Poutrincourt & ses gens sortant de la barque pour
venir à terre. Lors ladite chaloupe accrochée, Neptune commence ainsi.

NEPTVNE.

A RRETE, Sagamos, * arréte toy ici,
Et écoutes vn Dieu qui a de toy souci.
Si tu ne me conois, Saturne fut mon pere,
Je suis de Iupiter & de Pluton le frere.

*C'est vn
mot de
Sauvage,
qui signi-
fie Capi-
taine.

B

Fig. 17. Title page of *Le Théâtre de Neptune en la Nouvelle-France*, 1612 edition. The verse
at the top of the page is the last stanza of the previous poem in *Les Muses de la Nouvelle-
France*: "Adieu aux Francois Retournans de la Nouvelle-France en la France Gaulloise. Du
25 d'Aoust 1606," Lescarbot's farewell to his compatriots who returned to France at the
same time as Poutrincourt's expedition left for its explorations down the coast.

Le Théâtre de Neptune en la Nouvelle-France

Marc Lescarbot (1606)

Representé sur les flots du Port Royal le quatorziéme de Novembre mille six cens six, au retour du Sieur de Poutrincourt du païs des Armouchiquois.

Neptune commence revétu d'un voile de couleur bleuë, & de brodequins, ayant la chevelure & la barbe longues & chenuës, tenant son Trident en main, assis sur son chariot paré de ses couleurs: ledit chariot trainé sur les ondes par six Tritons jusques à l'abord de la chaloupe où s'étoit mis ledit Sieur de Poutrincourt & ses gens sortant de la barque pour venir à terre. Lors ladite chaloupe accrochée, Neptune commence ainsi.

NEPTUNE

ARRETE, *Sagamos*,[1] arréte-toy ici,
Et regardes un Dieu qui a de toy souci.
Si tu ne me conois, Saturne fut mon pere,
Je suis de Jupiter & de Pluton le frere.
Entre nous trois jadis fut parti l'Univers,
Jupiter eut le ciel, Pluton eut les Enfers,
Et moy plus hazardeux eu la mer en partage,
Et le gouvernement de ce moite heritage.
NEPTUNE c'est mon nom, Neptune l'un des Dieux
Qui a plus de pouvoir souz la voute des cieux.
 Si l'homme veut avoir une heureuse fortune
Il lui faut implorer le secours de Neptune.
Car celui qui chez soy demeure cazanier
Merite seulement le nom de cuisinier.
 Je fay que le Flamen en peu de temps chemine

---

1. SAGAMOS – C'est un mot de Sauvage, qui signifie Capitaine.

Aussi-tot que le vent jusques dedans la Chine.
Je fay que l'homme peut, porté dessus mes eaux,
D'un autre pole voir les inconuz flambeaux,
Et les bornes franchir de la Zone torride,
Ou bouïllonnent les flots de l'element liquide.
Sans moy le Roy François[2] d'un superbe elephant
N'eust du Persan receu le present triumphant:
Et encores sans moy onc les François gendarmes
Es terres du Levant n'eussent planté leurs armes.
Sans moy le Portugais hazardeux sur mes flots
Sans renom croupiroit dans ses rives enclos,
Et n'auroit enlevé les beautez de l'Aurore
Que le monde insensé folatrement adore.
Bref sans moy le marchant, pilote, marinier
Seroit en sa maison comme dans un panier
Sans à-peine pouvoir sortir de sa province.
Un Prince ne pourroit secourir l'autre Prince
Que j'auroy separé de mes profondes eaux.
Et toy-même sans moy aprés tant d'actes beaux
Que tu as exploités en la Françoise guerre,
N'eusses eu le plaisir d'aborder cette terre.
C'est moy qui sur mon dos ay tes vaisseaux porté
Quand de me visiter tu as eu volonté.
Et nagueres encor c'est moy qui de la Parque
Ay cent fois garenti toy, les tiens, & ta barque.
Ainsi je veux toujours seconder tes desseins,
Ainsi je ne veux point que tes effortz soient vains,
Puis que si constamment tu as eu le courage,
De venir de si loin rechercher ce rivage,
Pour établir ici un Royaume François,
Et y faire garder mes statuts & mes loix.
  Par mon sacré Trident, par mon sceptre je jure
Que de favoriser ton projet j'auray cure,
Et oncques je n'auray en moy-méme repos
Qu'en tout cet environ je ne voye mes flots
Ahanner souz le faix de dix milles navires
Qui facent d'un clin d'oeil tout ce que tu desires.
  Va donc heureusement, & poursui ton chemin

2. ROY FRANÇOIS – Charlemagne.

Où le sort te conduit: car je voy le destin
Preparer à la France un florissant Empire
En ce monde nouveau, qui bien loin fera bruire
Le renom immortel de De Monts & de toy
Souz le regne puissant de HENRY vôtre Roy.

Neptune ayant achevé, une trompete commence à éclater hautement & encourager les Tritons à faire de même. Ce-pendant le sieur de Poutrincourt tenoit son epée nuë en main, laquelle il ne remit point au fourreau jusques à ce que les Tritons eurent prononcé comme s'ensuit.

PREMIER TRITON

Tu peux (grand *Sagamos*) tu peux te dire heureux
Puisqu'un Dieu te promet favorable assistance
En l'affaire important que d'un coeur vigoureux
Hardi tu entreprens, forçant la violence
D'Æole, qui toujours inconstant & leger,
Tantot *adesquidés*,[3] tantot poussé d'envie,
Veut te precipiter, & les tiens au danger.
    Neptune est un grand Dieu, qui cette jalousie
Fera comme fumée en l'air évanouïr:
Et nous ses postillons, malgré l'effort d'Æole,
Ferons en toutes parts de ton courage ouïr
Le renom, qui des-ja en toutes terres vole.

DEUXIEME TRITON

Si Jupiter est Roy és cieux
Pour gouverner ça bas les hommes,
Neptune aussi l'est en ces lieux
Pour méme effect; & nous qui sommes
Ses suppos, avons grand desir
De voir le temps & la journée
Qu'ayes de tes travaux plaisir
Apres ta course terminée
Afin qu'en ces côtes ici
Bien-tot retentisse la gloire
Du puissant Neptune: & qu'ainsi
Tu eternises ta memoire.

---

3. ADESQUIDÉS – Mot de Sauvage, qui signifie Ami.

TROISIEME TRITON

France, tu as occasion
De loüer la devotion
De tes enfants dont le courage
Se montre plus grand en cet âge
Qu'il ne fit onc és siecles vieux,
Etans ardemment curieux
De faire éclater tes loüanges
Jusques aux peuples plus étranges,
Et graver ton los immortel
Méme souz ce monde mortel.
   Ayde doncques & favorise
Une si louable entreprise,
Neptune s'offre à ton secours
Qui les tiens maintiendra toujours
Contre toute l'humaine force,
Si quelqu'un contre toy s'efforce.
"Il ne faut jamais rejetter
Le bien qu'un Dieu nous veut preter."

QUATRIEME TRITON

Celui qui point ne se hazarde
Montre qu'il a l'ame coüarde
Mais celui qui d'un brave coeur
Méprise des flots la fureur
Pour un sujet rempli de gloire
Fait à chacun aisément croire
Que de courage & de vertu
Il est tout ceint & revetu,
Et qu'il ne veut que le silence
Tienne son nom en oubliance.
   Ainsi ton nom (grand *Sagamos*)
Retentira dessus les flots
D'or-en-avant, quand dessus l'onde
Tu découvres ce nouveau monde,
Et y plantes le nom François,
Et la Majesté de tes Rois.

CINQUIEME TRITON

Un Gascon prononça ces vers à peu prés à sa langue.

Sabets aquo que volio diro,
Aqueste Neptune bieillart
L'autre jou faisio del bragart,
Et comme un bergalant se miro.
    N'agaires que fasio l'amou,
Et baisavo une jeune hillo
Qu'ero plan polide & gentillo,
Et la cerquavo quandejou.
    Bezets, ne vous fizets pas trop
En aquels gens de barbos grisos,
Car en aqueles entreprisos
Els ban lou trot & lou galop.

SIXIEME TRITON

Vive HENRY le grand Roy des François
Qui maintenant fait vivre souz ses loix
Les nations de sa Nouvelle-France,
Et souz lequel nous avons esperance
De voir bien-tot Neptune reveré
Autant ici qu'oncq il fut honoré
Par ses sujets sur le Gaullois rivage,
Et en tous lieux où le brave courage
De leurs ayeuls jadis les a porté.
Neptune aussi fera de son côté
Que leurs neveux s'employans sans féintise
A l'ornement de leur belle entreprise,
Tous leurs desseins il favorisera,
Et prosperer sur ses eaux il fera.

Cela fait, Neptune s'équarte un petit pour faire place à un canot, dans lequel étoient quatre Sauvages, qui s'approcherent apportans chacun un present audit Poutrincourt.[4]

---

4. [Every edition but that of 1618 reads "sieur de Poutrincourt." —JW]

PREMIER SAUVAGE

Le premier Sauvage offre un quartier d'Ellan ou Orignac, disant ainsi:

De la part des peuples Sauvages
Qui environnent ces païs
Nous venons rendre les homages
Deuz aux sacrées Fleur-de-lis
Es mains de toy, qui de ton Prince
Representes la Majesté,
Attendans que cette province
Faces florir en pieté,
En moeurs civils, & toute chose
Qui sert à l'établissement
De ce qui est beau, & repose
En un Royal gouvernement.
Sagamos, si en nos services
Tu as quelque devotion,
A toy en faisons sacrifices
Et à ta generation.
  Noz moyens sont un peu de chasse,
Que d'un coeur entier nous t'offrons,
Et vivre toujours en ta grace
C'est tout ce que nous desirons.

DEUXIEME SAUVAGE

Le deuxiesme Sauvage tenant son arc & sa fleche en main, donne pour son present des peaux de Castors, disant:

Voici la main, l'arc, & la fleche
Qui ont fait la mortele breche
En l'animal de qui la peau
Pourra servir d'un bon manteau
(Grand *Sagamos*) à ta hautesse.
  Reçoy donc de ma petitesse
Cette offrande qu'à ta grandeur
J'offre du meilleur de mon coeur.

TROISIEME SAUVAGE

Le troisiéme Sauvage offre des **Matachiaz,** *c'est à dire, echarpes, &*
brasselets faits de la main de sa maitresse, disant:

Ce n'est seulement en France
Que commande Cupidon,
Mais en la Nouvelle-France,
Comme entre vous, son brandon
Il allume, & de ses flammes
Il rotit noz pauvres ames,
Et fait planter le bourdon.
    Ma maitresse ayant nouvelle
Que tu devois arriver,
M'a dit que pour l'amour d'elle
J'eusse à te venir trouver,
Et qu'offrande je te fisse
De ce petit exercice
Que sa main à sceu ouvrer.
    Reçoy doncques d'allegresse
Ce present que je t'adresse
Tout rempli de gentillesse
Pour l'amour de ma maitresse
Qui est ores en détresse
Et n'aura point de liesse
Si d'une prompte vitesse
Je ne lui di la caresse
Que m'aura fait ta hautesse.

QUATRIEME SAUVAGE

Le quatriéme Sauvage n'ayant heureusement chassé par les bois, se
presente avec un harpon en main, & aprés ses excuses faites, dit qu'il
s'en va à la péche.

SAGAMOS, pardonne moy
Si je viens en telle sorte,
Si me presentant à toy
Quelque present je n'apporte.

Fortune n'est pas toujours
Aux bons chasseurs favorable,
C'est pourquoy ayant recours
A un maitre plus traitable,
Aprés avoir maintefois
Invoqué cette Fortune
Brossant par l'epés des bois,
Je m'en vay suivre Neptune.
    Que Diane en ses foréts
Ceux qu'elle voudra caresse,
Je n'ay que trop de regrets
D'avoir perdu ma jeunesse
A la suivre par les vaux,
Par les bois & par les plaines
Avecque mille travaux,
Souz des esperances vaines.
    Maintenant je m'en vay voir
Par cette côte marine
Si je pourray point avoir
Dequoy fournir ta cuisine:
Et cependant si tu as
Quelque part en ta chaloupe
Un peu de *caracona*,[5]
Fournis-en moy & ma troupe.

Aprés que Neptune eut eté remercié par le sieur de Poutrincourt de ses offres au bien de la France, les Sauvages le furent semblablement de leur bonne volonté & devotion; & invitez de venir au fort Royal prendre du caracona. *A l'instant la troupe de Neptune chante en Musique à quatre parties ce qui s'ensuit.*

Vray Neptune donne nous
Contre tes flots asseurance,
Et fay que nous puissions tous
Un jour nous revoir en France.

La Musique achevée, la trompette sonne derechef, & chacun prend sa route diversement: les Canons bourdonnent de toutes parts, & semble à ce tonnerre que Proserpine soit en travail d'enfant: ceci causé par la multiplicité des Echoz que les côtaux s'envoient les uns aux autres, lesquels durent plus d'un quart d'heure.

---

5. CARACONA – C'est du pain.

Le Sieur de Poutrincourt arrivé prés du Fort Royal, un compagnon de gaillarde humeur qui l'attendoit de pié ferme, dit ce qui s'ensuit.

Aprés avoir long temps (*Sagamos*) desiré
Ton retour en ce lieu, en fin le ciel iré
A eu pitié de nous, & nous montrant ta face,
Nous a favorisé d'une incroyable grace.
    Sus doncques rotisseurs, depensiers, cuisiniers,
Marmitons, patissiers, fricasseurs, taverniers,
Mettez dessus dessouz pots & plats & cuisine,
Qu'on baille à ces gens ci chacun sa quarte pleine,
Je les voy alterez *sicut terra sine aqua.*
Garson depeche-toy, baille à chacun son K.
Cuisiniers, ces canars sont-ils point à la broche?
Qu'on tuë ces poulets, que cette oye on embroche,
Voici venir à nous force bons compagnons
Autant deliberez des dents que des roignons.
Entrez dedans, Messieurs, pour vôtre bien-venuë,
Qu'avant boire chacun hautement éternuë,
A fin de decharger toutes froides humeurs
Et remplir voz cerveaux de plus douces vapeurs.

Je prie le Lecteur excuser si ces rhimes ne sont si bien limées que les hommes delicats pourroient desirer. Elles ont eté faites à la hate. Mais neantmoins je les ay voulu inserer ici, tant pour-ce qu'elles servent à nôtre Histoire, que pour montrer que nous vivions joyeusement. Le surplus de cette action se peut voir à la fin du chap. 16, liv. 4, de mon Histoire de la Nouvelle-France.

Fig. 18. Lescarbot's map of Port Royal, published in the *Histoire*, 1609. Note the indigenous wildlife on land and sea.

The Theatre of Neptune in New France

Trans. Harriette Taber Richardson (1927)

Dramatis Personæ

NEPTUNE, The Sea God
FIRST TRITON
SECOND TRITON
THIRD TRITON
FOURTH TRITON
FIFTH TRITON, A Gascon
SIXTH TRITON
FOUR SAVAGES
THE GAY COMPANION
JEAN DE BIENCOURT, Sieur de Poutrincourt

Gentlemen	Sailor	Trumpeters
Surgeons	Laborers	Cooks
Savages		

Place
Before the Habitation in the Harbor of Port Royal, Acadia, New France

Scene
On the waves of Port Royal Harbor
In the shallop and canoe
At the landing place before the Habitation

Time
In the reign of Henri of Navarre

Explorers arriving in the shallop from Port Fortuné:*

JEAN DE BIENCOURT, Sieur de Poutrincourt, Baron St. Just, de
   Marsilly-sur-Seine, de Guibermensil, Chantenes, Dumensil, Vimeu,
   Baron of Saint-Just and Port Royal, Chevalier of the Order of the King
CHARLES DE BIENCOURT, fifteen or sixteen years of age, son of de
   Poutrincourt
SAMUEL CHAMPLAIN of Brouage, Royal Geographer
ROBERT DU PONT, son of Pontgravé
PIERRE AUGIBAUT, called Champdoré, pilot
LOUIS HEBERT, the worthy apothecary
DANIEL HAY, carpenter
MASTER STEPHEN, surgeon
JEAN DU VAL, locksmith
ESTIENNE, valet to de Poutrincourt
A dying man, unnamed

Present as audience or possibly as actors on the shore:

RALLEAU, secretary to Sieur de Monts
Noblemen:
   SIEUR DE BOULLET, future brother-in-law to Champlain
   FOLGERÉ DE VITRÍ
   LE FÉVRE of Retel
   DE NOYES
FRANÇOIS ARDAMIN, provider of birds and game for the household
LA TAILLE
MICQUELET
MEMBERTOU, Sagamos of Souriquois, his family and people

---

* These names are gathered from Lescarbot's *History of New France* and Champlain's *Voyages*,
especially the edition of 1613 of the latter.

The Theatre of Neptune in New France

Presented upon the waves of Port Royal the fourteenth day of November, sixteen hundred and six, upon the return of Sieur de Poutrincourt from the Armouchiquois country.

Neptune speaks first robed in a veil of blue, with buskins, gray hair and a beard worn long. He holds his trident in his hand and is seated upon his chariot adorned with varied colors. The chariot is drawn over the waves by six Tritons and so they come in state to the side of the shallop in which Sieur de Poutrincourt is sitting with his company ready to leave the boat and go ashore. As the shallop grapples, Neptune speaks as follows.

NEPTUNE

HAIL to you, Sagamos,[1] rest and remain awhile!
Come, listen to a God who welcomes with a smile!
And if you know me not, great Saturn was my sire,
Brother am I to Jove, and Pluto, God of fire.
Of old the world was held by us in equal part,
Jove rules the windy sky, Pluto the flaming heart,
And I command the sea, the mighty waves my care.
Where deepest danger lurks is my appointed share.
Neptune is my dread name, Neptune, Sea-lord am I,
Most powerful of Gods, beneath the vaulting sky.
  If a man has the wish and a will to succeed
The help of Neptune he must make bold to plead,
For he who is house-bound and never will look
Outside, merits chiefly the name of a cook.

---

1. SAGAMOS – This is a savage word meaning Captain.

I order that the Fleming shall reach the China Sea,
With favoring wind and wave made fortunate through me.
I order that the man who dares my crested heights,
Shall see another pole and unknown, vivid lights.
Or he may cross the borders of the wide and torrid zone,
Where elemental waters steam, deserted and alone.
I led to a French King,[2] enthroned and jubilant,
The gift from jewelled Persia, of a princely elephant.
And more, without my help, the gallant French gendarmes,
In the countries of the East had never planted arms.
Without my power, the Portuguese, who venture any weather,
Were cooped within their coasts, lost to glory altogether,
And the beauties of Aurora had never been unfurled,
To be adored with madness, throughout the foolish world.
In brief, without Neptune, the merchant, pilot, sailor,
Would each remain at home, like a veritable tailor.
And unless he had the power to sail out from his land,
No Prince could succor Prince, his drawn sword in his hand.
For I can part kings widely with the depths of my gray seas,
And you, without Neptune, had never fought with ease
Nor performed your own brave deeds in the terrible French war;
Nor had you landed here, after sailing from afar!
It is I, on my wide back, your toy ships have carried,
When your wish to visit me in a little, you have tarried.
I overpowered Fate and won from her dread lip
One hundred guarantees for you and your ship.
So, I will always send good winds to fill your sail.
The day will never dawn when your splendid plans shall fail.
Fine courage you have had, that has led you to explore
With a bold constancy this strange and fog-bound shore,
That you may here establish a wide realm for France
And carefully may guard my laws from all mischance.
    By my sacred trident, by my sceptre, I now swear
That to favor this high project shall be my happy care!
Even though you override me I shall never take my rest,
Until you bring the burden and the toil to my breast,
Of ten thousand busy ships that with noisy hue and cry

---

2. FRENCH KING – Charlemagne. [Note to 1618 Edition. In the year 801 Harun-al-Rachid exchanged gifts with Charlemagne.]

Shall carry out your orders in the twinkling of an eye.
   Go, then, with happiness, and follow on your way
Where ever fortune leads you, since I foresee the day,
When a prosperous domain you will prepare for France
In this fair, new world and the future will enhance
The glory of de Monts, so too, your name shall ring
Immortal in the reign of Henry—your great king.

Neptune having finished speaking, a trumpet sounds loudly, to encourage the Tritons to do the same. In the meantime Sieur de Poutrincourt takes his sword in his hand which he does not replace in the scabbard until the Tritons have spoken as follows:

FIRST TRITON

By right, great SAGAMOS, you name your luck as rare,
Because a fostering god has promised you his aid
In this important work, wherein with dauntless care
And hardy venturing, your conquest bold is made
Over strong Æolus. He, changing and unstable,
Often Adesquides,[3] at times by envy driven,
To harm you and your friends has found himself unable.
   Our powerful Neptune, this jealousy has riven,
And scattered as light smoke, it vanishes on high.
We, Tritons, his postillions, despite Eolian hate,
Triumphantly your courage to outer shores will cry,
Although your fame already has flown through every state.

SECOND TRITON

If Jupiter is lord of skies
And governs men upon the earth,
On sea, the realm of Neptune lies
With equal part and we by birth
His Tritons are. Our greatest pleasure
And wish to see the hour and day
Your arduous task may bring fair leisure
And your cruise end so glad a way
That these wild coasts, this fragrant land

---

3. ADESQUIDES – A savage word that signifies Friend.

May long reëcho with the glory
Of proud Neptune! Thus, you shall stand
And place your name in deathless story!

THIRD TRITON

France, with fairest reason
Your praises are in season
For sons whose love and loyal courage
Appear more grandly in our age
Than in the centuries of old.
Through eager care and action bold
They seek to honor you and place
In farthest lands, to a strange race,
The codes of your immortal law
That mortal world shall hold in awe.
    Then give your help and prospering favor
Unto so wonderful a labor!
Neptune, himself, gives godlike power
To you and yours in this great hour.
No human force can bring you harm
Whatever threat may bring alarm
"For man should never lose or spend
Good fortune that a god shall send."

FOURTH TRITON

The man who dares not take a chance
Is called a coward, at a glance.
Yet he who with brave heart is born,
Holding the furious waves in scorn,
Who, on high quest, will strive for glory,
Wins all the world to trust the story
That courage and civility
Enforce in him authority.
This man will never wish his name
In silence wrapped and lost to fame.
Thus, Sagamos, your name shall ring
Above the wide seas echoing,
More surely, since beyond the deep

You find an unknown world asleep.
You bind thereon the name of France,
Her kingly power and circumstance.

FIFTH TRITON

A Gascon pronounces these verses after his own dialect.

Listen, to what I want to say
About dat high flown God Neptune!
I caught de peacock—t'odder day
Carryin' on lak one dragoon.

    Don't be surprised dat he mak love,
An' kissed one pretty, leetle girl;
Dat he were soft, lak one beeg dove.
Wid hees whole heart he hunt dat pearl.

    Look out, you don' trusts too queek,
De peoples wid long beards, all gray;
For in dis game, dey know one treek,
Dey trot one while, den race away.

SIXTH TRITON

Hail, King of France, Henry the Great!
Under your law New France holds her state.
New nations are yours, rich in your name,
And we, the bold Tritons, hope that the fame
Of Neptune, in reverence, here you may hold
High, as when in the days of old
The God was praised and worshipped by all
The dwellers upon the coasts of Gaul;
In regions where courage and hardiest daring
Called heroes abroad to fearless sea-faring.
These, their descendants, for unselfish labor
Our God will cherish in his special favor
And prosper the end of their splendid emprise
Upon the great waves where his empire lies.

After this, Neptune withdraws a little to give place to a canoe, in which are four Indians who approach, each bearing a present to Sieur de Poutrincourt.

FIRST INDIAN

The first Indian offers a quarter of a moose or deer, speaking as follows:

In the name of the peoples uncouth
Whose homeland is bound by their seas,
We come to give our vows, in truth,
Unto the sacred Fleur-de-lis
Unfurling from your faithful hand.
You act in princely majesty,
Watchful to tend in this rude land
The habit of sweet piety
And gentler ways, to foster all
That should secure establishment
Of common good, or what may fall
To build a Royal Government.
So, Sagamos, in every act
You find us friends, in verity,
And true devotion in our pact
With you and your posterity.
   Our little talent in the chase
We beg you use, from hearts entire.
To live forever in your grace
Is all our wish, our whole desire.

SECOND INDIAN

The second Indian holding his bow and arrow in hand gives for his present some beaver skins, saying:

Here is the hand, the arrow and bow
That pierced the hide and dealt the blow
Upon this beast, whose furry skin
Shall serve as a coat and wrap therein
Great Sagamos, your lordly self.
Accept, high sir, this woodland pelf
Rifled by one, so low in part.
The humble gift, I offer from my heart.

THIRD INDIAN

The third Indian offers Matachiaz,[4] that is to say, a scarf and bracelets made by the hand of his lady love, saying:

'Tis not alone in France
That Cupidon commands
Throughout this young new France
As in your world he stands
And lights his torch with flame,
To heat our hearts, his game.
So plants he his light wands.

    My mistress heard the news that sped
As herald you were to arrive,
For very love of her she pled
That I should find you and contrive
To offer you her humble duty,
Through this small gift of dainty beauty
Her skilful hand has made alive.

    Receive, kind sir, with cheerfulness
This gift to you that I address!
A work all wrought with gentleness,
In courtesy of my mistress.
She would be sad and in distress
And lose her pretty playfulness
If promptly and with nimbleness,
I may not tell her of a kindness
Shown to me, here, your noble highness.

FOURTH INDIAN

The fourth Indian, having been unfortunate in his hunting, presents himself with a harpoon in hand and after his excuses have been made says that he is going to fish.

Sagamos, pardon me,
If before you, here, I stand,
Present, in this company,
With no present in my hand.

---

4. MATACHIAZ – An Indian word for porcupine-quill or bead embroidery.

Fortune is not always kind
Her good hunters cheering!
For this reason I must find
Another field—I'm fearing.
For, through many useless days
I invoked frail Fortune,
Her wooden swords I toss away
To follow after Neptune.
Let Dian hold in sylvan shade
Those she would caress, in truth,
My regrets will never fade
That I lost my lusty youth
And her clumsy cattle chased
Over hills[5] and near-by plain;
Many a hundred trails I traced
And always found my hopes were vain.
    Now, I am about to try
My luck upon this rocky coast.
Perchance upon the shore will lie
Something for your cook to roast.
And now, monseigneur, if you see
Within the locker of your sloop
Some caraconas,[6] give to me
And I will share it with my troop.

After Neptune had been thanked by Sieur de Poutrincourt for his offers toward the good of France, the Indians were also thanked for their good wishes and devotion, and they were invited to come to Fort Royal and to take bread. At this moment the troupe of Neptune sings in music of four parts the verse that follows.

FOUR PART SONG

Give us your pledge, great God Neptune,
Against wild ocean arrogance.
And grant us all, as your high boon
That we may meet again in France.

---

5. [The Edition of 1618 has the word *bois* (woods) for *monts* (hills).] 6. CARACONAS – i.e. bread. [This custom of bread-giving was first observed by Lescarbot at Canso in 1606.]

The music having finished, the trumpets sounded again and each man took his several way. The cannons broke forth on all sides and it seemed as though Proserpine were in birth pangs for her child. This effect was caused by the innumerable echoes sent back against one another from these hills and which continued for a quarter of an hour. The Sieur de Poutrincourt having arrived before Fort Royal habitation, a companion in a merry mood who was waiting for him patiently, spoke as follows:

> Sagamos, the days of loneliness are past.
> An angry heaven ordains your safe return at last,
> And with relenting pity has shown to us your face,
> Dispersing all our care with kind, surprising grace.
> Come, then, chefs, cooks, and boys—all you who make good cheer.
> Scullions and pastry cooks, let soup and roast appear,
> Ransack the kitchen shelves, fill every pot and pan
> And draw his own good portion[7] for every eager man!
> I see the men are thirsty, SICUT TERRA, SINE AQUA[8]
> Come, hurry boy, and pour for each his beaded measure.
> Bestir yourselves, be brisk. Are the ducks on the spit?
> What fowl have lost their heads? The goose, who cares for it?
> Hither have sailed to us a band of comrades rare;
> Let portions and their hunger be matched with equal care.
> Enter within, messires, your welcome gaily seize,
> Let each man drain his cup! Let each man strongly sneeze!
> That never a frosty humor his person may contain
> And only sweetest vapors may crowd his merry brain.

I ask the reader to excuse these rhymes if they are not as well polished as a well-bred man would wish. They were made in haste. But nevertheless I have a wish to insert them here because they serve as a part of our history and to show that we lived joyously. The further part of the action may be seen at the end of Chapter 16, book 4, of my History of New France.

---

7. [The portion was three pints per person.] 8. [From the Vulgate Latin Bible, Psalms 142:6: *anima mea sicut terra sine aqua tibi* (My soul is as earth without water unto thee). —JW]

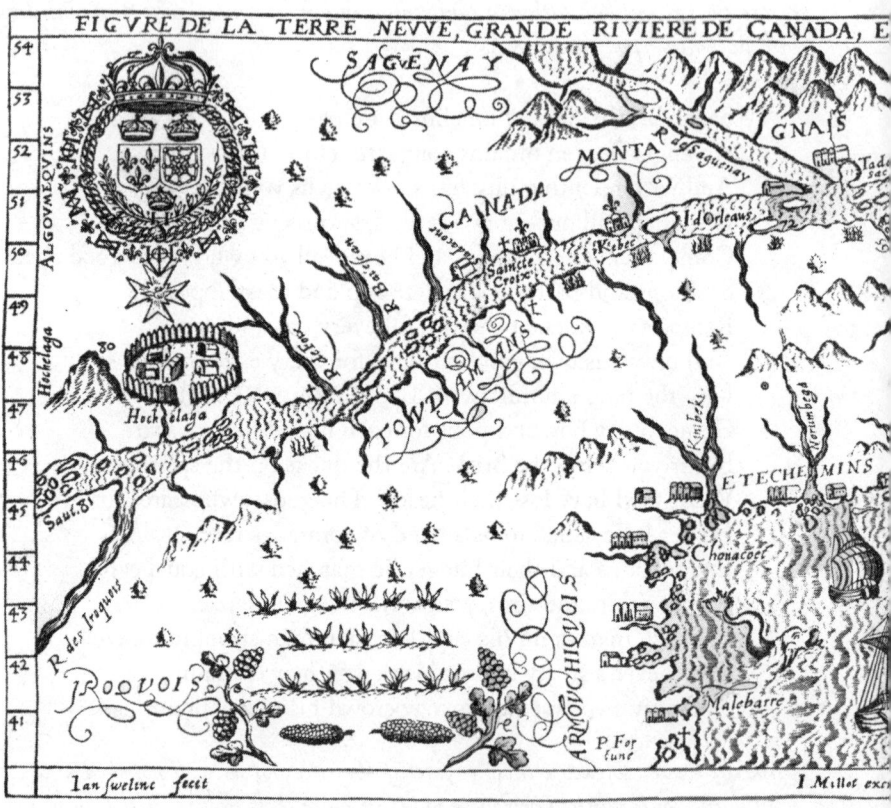

Fig. 19. Lescarbot's map of New France, from his *Histoire* (1609), featuring Newfoundland (Terre Neuve), the Gulf of St. Lawrence (Golfe de Canada), the St. Lawrence River (La grande Rivière de Canada), and in the central foreground the territory of the Souriquois, and Port Royal: "I have therefore placed at the beginning of this third book the map of the great river and gulf of Canada, with the countries and islands which surround it, whereunto the reader will in imagination be carried when he sees thereon the places marked by their names" (II:3).

The Theatre of Neptune in New France

Trans. Eugene Benson and Renate Benson (1982)

Presented upon the waves of Port Royal on the fourteenth of November, sixteen hundred and six, on the return of Sieur de Poutrincourt from the country of the Armouchiquois.

Neptune, dressed in a blue cloak, wearing buskins, with long hoary hair and beard, speaks first. Trident in hand he is seated on his chariot which is decorated with his colours: the chariot is drawn on the waves by six Tritons to the side of the shallop where Sieur de Poutrincourt and his entourage having waited are now ready to leave the boat and go ashore. After the shallop is coupled, Neptune begins as follows.

NEPTUNE

HALT, Sagamos,[1] stop here,
And behold a God who has care for you.
In case you do not know me, Saturn was my father,
And I am the brother of Jupiter and Pluto.
Once upon a time the Universe was divided among us three;
Jupiter received the sky, Pluto the Underworld,
And I, being more foolhardy, received the sea,
And the government of this moist inheritance.
NEPTUNE is my name, Neptune one of the Gods,
The most powerful beneath the heavens' vault.
    If a man wants a lucky fate
He must implore the help of Neptune,
Because he who is a stay-at-home
Deserves to be called only by the name of a cook.

---

1. SAGAMOS – An Indian word meaning Captain.

I arrange it that the Fleming travels
As swiftly as the wind as far as China.
I make it happen that a man, carried on my waves,
Can see from another pole unknown stars,
And can cross the borders of the torrid zone
Where the waves of the liquid element foam.
Without me the French King would not have received
The triumphant gift of a superb elephant from Persia:
And, furthermore, without me the French soldiers
Would not have planted their arms in the countries of the Orient.
Without me the Portuguese, venturing on my waves,
Would have wallowed without glory on their enclosed banks,
And would not have carried away the treasures of the East
Which the mad world foolishly adores.
In short, without me, the merchant, the pilot, the sailor
Would be home-bound as if in a prison
With little chance of escaping from his province.
Princes whom I would have separated
Because of my deep waters could not come to the help of each other.
Without me you too would not have had the pleasure
Of disembarking on this land after so many brilliant deeds
Which you performed in the French war.
It was I who carried your vessels on my back
When you cared to visit me.
Also, not long ago it was I who a hundred times
Defended you, your people, and your boat against Fate.
So, I will always help you in your plans
Because I do not want your efforts to be in vain,
And because you have always had the courage
To journey from so far away to explore this shore
In order to establish a French domain here
And have my status and my laws respected.
    I swear by my sacred Trident, my sceptre,
That I will always support your enterprises.
And I will never rest
Until I see my waves in this area
Pant under the weight of ten thousand ships
Which in the twinkling of an eye do whatever you want.

Therefore, go forth joyously and follow the path
Where destiny guides you, because I see Fate
Preparing a flourishing Empire for France
In this new world which in the future will proclaim
The immortal renown of De Monts, and of you too,
Under the mighty reign of HENRY, your King.

After Neptune has finished speaking, a trumpet sounds loudly encouraging the Tritons to do the same. Meanwhile Sieur de Poutrincourt holds his sword in his hands which he does not replace in the scabbard until the Tritons have spoken as follows.

FIRST TRITON

You can call yourself happy (great Sagamos)
Because a God promises you favourable assistance
In the important matter which you are undertaking
With a spirited and daring heart; He tempers the violence
Of Aeolus who, always inconstant and fickle,
At times *adesquidés*,[2] at times driven by envy,
Wants to throw you and your people into danger.
    Neptune is a powerful God who will make
This jealousy vanish in the air like smoke.
And we, his postillions, despite the efforts of Aeolus,
Will everywhere proclaim the fame of your courage
Which already flies through all countries.

SECOND TRITON

If Jupiter is King of the skies
Governing men below,
Neptune is also King in these places,
With equal power; and we who are
His instruments have a great wish
To see the time and the day
When you will derive pleasure from your task
After your journey is done,
So that soon in these coasts here
The glory of the mighty Neptune may resound:
And so your memory is eternalized.

---

2. ADESQUIDÉS – An Indian word meaning Friend.

THIRD TRITON

France, you have reason
To praise the devotion
Of your children whose courage
Reveals itself more grandly in this age
Than ever it did in past centuries.
They are keenly interested
In trumpeting your praises abroad
To the most unknown of peoples,
And in engraving your immortal destiny
Throughout the mortal world.
   Therefore, help and support
Such a praiseworthy enterprise.
Neptune offers you his own assistance
Which will always support you and yours
Against all human power
In case someone should threaten you.
"We must never reject
The gift which a God wishes to grant us."

FOURTH TRITON

The man who doesn't take a risk
Shows that he has the soul of a coward.
But he who with a brave heart
Defies the fury of the waves
For a glorious enterprise
Makes everyone easily believe
That he is belted and clothed
In courage and virtue,
And that he does not wish silence
To veil his name in oblivion.
   Therefore your name (great Sagamos)
Will henceforth reverberate above the waves
When on the deep
You discover this new world

And plant the name of France
And the Majesty of your Kings.

FIFTH TRITON

A Gascon speaks these verses in his own dialect.

Hear ye what I wish to say:
That old fellow, Neptune,
Bragged loudly the other day
Admiring himself like a real ladies' man.
  —Once I made love
And kissed a young wench
Who was very polite and gentle;
I frequented her company every day—
  Young lovers, don't trust too much
Those who have grey beards,
Because in these adventures
They trot slowly, then off they gallop!

SIXTH TRITON

Long live HENRY the great King of France
Who now has living under his laws
The nations of his New France,
Under whom we hope
Soon to see Neptune held in reverence
As much here as he once was honoured
By his subjects on the shores of Gaul,
And in all those places where the bravery and courage
Of their ancestors once led them.
Neptune, for his part, will always see
That their descendants employ themselves industriously
Embellishing this wonderful enterprise;
He will favour all their plans
And make them flourish on his waters.

This done, Neptune steps aside a little to make room for a canoe in which are four Indians who approach, each bringing a gift to Sieur de Poutrincourt.

FIRST INDIAN

The first Indian offers a quarter of an elk or moose, speaking as follows.

On behalf of the Indian peoples
Who inhabit these countries,
We come to render their homage
To the sacred Fleur-de-lis
In your hands, you who represent
The Majesty of your Prince;
Hoping that this province
Will flourish in piety,
In civil customs, and in everything
Which is of service in establishing
That which is gracious
And rests in Royal governance.
Sagamos, if you have any faith
In our services,
Then we will devote ourselves to you
And to your descendants.
   We offer whole-heartedly our skills
Which lie only in hunting,
And all we desire
Is to live forever in your favour.

SECOND INDIAN

The second Indian, holding his bow and arrow in his hand, gives some beaver skins as his present, saying:

Here is the hand, the bow and the arrow
Which have inflicted the mortal wound
On this animal whose skin
Should serve (Great Sagamos)
As a warm coat for your Highness.
   Accept, therefore, from one who is so unimportant
This offering which I present to your Highness
From the bottom of my heart.

THIRD INDIAN

The third Indian offers Matachiaz, that is, sashes and bracelets made by the hand of his mistress, saying:

It is not only in France
That Cupid reigns,
But also in New France.
As with you he also lights
His firebrand here; and with his flames
He scorches our poor souls
And plants there his flag.
    My mistress, when she heard the news
That you were to arrive,
Told me that for love of her
I must come seeking you,
And that I must make you gifts
Of this little work
Which her skilled hand wrought.
    Therefore, accept gladly—
For the love of my mistress—
This present made with such affection
Which I offer you;
For she is now in distress
And will not be happy
Unless I tell her promptly
Of the kindness which your Highness has done me.

FOURTH INDIAN

The fourth Indian, having hunted unsuccessfully in the woods, presents himself with a harpoon in hand and, after his excuses have been made, announces that he is going fishing.

SAGAMOS, pardon me
If I come in this manner,
If, while presenting myself to you,
I do not bring you any gifts.
Fortune is not always favourable

To good hunters;
That is why, having now recourse
To a more friendly master,
And after having many times
When brushing through the thickets of the woods
Invoked this Fortune,
I will now follow Neptune.
  May Diana in her forests
Cherish those whom she wants;
I, for my part, have too many regrets
Because of having lost my youth
While following her through the valleys
With a thousand labours
In vain hopes.
  Now I will search
Along this sea coast
To see whether I cannot find something
To provide for your kitchen:
And, if meanwhile, you have
Somewhere in your shallop
A little *caraconas*[3]
Give some to me and to my company.

After Neptune had been thanked by Sieur de Poutrincourt for his offers for the well being of France, the Indians were similarly thanked for their good will and loyalty and were invited to come to Fort Royal in order to break bread. At this moment Neptune's troupe sings a song in four parts, as follows.

Loyal Neptune, grant us
Security against your waves,
And grant that we will all be able
To meet again in France one day.

The Music finished, the trumpet sounds once more and every one takes his different route: the cannons boom from all sides and thunder as if Proserpine were in labour: this is caused by the multiplicity of echoes which the hills send back to each other. That lasts for more than a quarter of an hour.

---

3. CARACONAS – That is, bread.

Then Sieur de Poutrincourt having arrived near Port Royal, a companion of a jolly disposition, who had awaited him patiently, speaks as follows.

After having wished a long time (Sagamos)
For your return to this place, finally the angry sky
Now had pity on us and, showing us your face,
Bestows on us an incredible favour.
    Pay attention then grillers, waiters, cooks,
Kitchen hands, bakers, makers of fricassee, tavern keepers;
Turn the pots, plates and kitchen upside down!
Let's give to each of these gentlemen his full quart;
I see that they are thirsty, *sicut terra sine aqua*[4]
Boy, busy yourself, give each one his portion.
Cooks, are the ducks on the skewer yet?
Kill the chickens, put the goose on a spit,
Here come jolly good companions
As free with their teeth as with their kidneys.
Enter, Sirs, for your good pleasure.
Before drinking, let each one sneeze loudly
In order to discharge all cold humours,
And fill your brain with sweeter vapours.

I beg the reader to excuse me if these rhymes are not as well polished as an educated man would wish. They have been composed in haste. However, I wanted to insert them here that they might contribute to our History in addition to showing that we lived joyously. The rest of this story may be found at the end of Chapter 16, book 4, of my History of New France.

⌘

---

4. SICUT TERRA SINE AQUA – ["As earth without water," from the Vulgate Bible, Psalms 142: 6. —JW]

❧ Introduction ❧
The Masque of Blackness

The Eloquence of Masques, the Spectacle of State, *The Masque of Blackness*

In a discussion of Inigo Jones's theatrical designs, Stephen Orgel and Roy Strong assert, "Every masque is a ritual in which the society affirms its wisdom and asserts its control of its world and its destiny" (13). But not every masque uses the "production of wonder" (Orgel and Strong 10) enacted by its spectacle to articulate and reinforce its society's discourses of power as blatantly as do *The Theatre of Neptune in New France* and *The Masque of Blackness*. Ben Jonson and Inigo Jones's nautical masque, in contrast to Lescarbot's, was a fantastically aestheticized, hugely expensive production with make-believe boats on a make-believe sea in an indoor theatre. Yet despite these obvious differences and others that pertain to the particular conditions of its production at the behest of Queen Anne, *The Masque of Blackness* similarly utilized the sea god and his tritons as well as representations of Native peoples deferring to the imperial power, in this case Africans performed by the Queen herself and her elaborately costumed ladies in blackface make-up. Although the Queen may just have been playing at the exotic, it seems difficult to avoid the overt political implications of the masque's imperial rhetoric and domestication of blackness. It celebrates "Albion the fair," "Britannia, this blest isle," and the glory and power of King James, "Neptune's son who ruleth here." Oceanus himself is "proud to see [James] crowned / Above my waves." And Aethiopia, the African moon goddess, assures Niger, father of the continent's rivers, that his daughters have found their proper home under the sway of "Britannia, whose new name makes all tongues sing."

The Masque of Blackness was the first of many such theatrical collaborations between poet/playwright Jonson and artist/architect Jones that ended after a quarter-century with their famous quarrel over the comparative virtues of literature and spectacle, verbal poetry and physical design. In an extraordinarily dyspeptic attack in his 1631 poem "An Expostulation with Inigo Jones," Jonson mocks Jones's forms of invention and his claims for their primacy:

> O shows! Shows! Mighty shows!
> The eloquence of masques! What need of prose,
> Or verse, or sense, to express immortal you?
> You are the spectacle of state! 'Tis true ...

I am not concerned with the nature or details of their disagreement (for the standard explication of which, see Gordon 77–101). Beneath Jonson's sarcasm here lie some truths about the masque, which was indeed a theatrically eloquent form through which to express, explore, and in Jonson's case publicize the spectacle of the contemporary imperial state, its power and self-glorification. Introducing *The Masque of Blackness*, Jonson writes of the need to preserve the "honour and splendour of these spectacles" in his published text, to redeem from oblivion "these solemnities"—the same word Lescarbot used to describe his *Theatre of Neptune*.

Jonson first explains how, at the Queen's behest, the production was to be about "blackamoors" from the River Niger region. He then carefully details the extraordinary scene and elaborate costumes created by Jones: the landscape-curtain which fell to reveal an artificial sea with waves upon which tritons and sea-maids appeared, as well as Oceanus and Niger upon the backs of sea-horses, and the twelve daughters of Niger who entered in "a great concave shell like mother of pearl" which gave the illusion of sailing upon the artificial waves. (These, the masquers, were the Queen herself and her ladies, all in blackface, a scenario which offended at least one member of the audience, Dudley Carleton, who reported, "Theyr black faces, and hands which were painted and bare up to the elbowes, was a very lothsome sight" [qtd. in Jonson, ed. Herford and Simpson, X:449].) The daughters of Niger were accompanied by their twelve attendants, the Oceaniae, riding on the backs of sea-monsters. All of this scenery, this "bodily part, which was of Master Inigo Jones his design and act," was presented in illusionistic perspective, Jonson declares, using King James's throne ("the level of the state") as the point of reference, "which decorum made it more conspicuous." (See figs. 20 & 21.)

Jonson the poet then takes over. In the couplet form used throughout the verse, Niger explains to Oceanus why he and his daughters have come so far west. "[T]he Ethiops," once "as fair / As other dames," are "now black with black despair," their complexions having been darkened by the sun. A reflection in a lake told them that a cure for their ills could be found in a land whose name ends in –*tania*, graced by "a greater light" than the sun's. They

Fig. 20. "The Masquer: A Daughter of Niger," one of Inigo Jones's watercolour costume designs for *The Masque of Blackness*. Devonshire Collection, Chatsworth. Reproduced by permission of the Duke of Devonshire and the Trustees of the Chatsworth Settlement. Photograph: Photographic Survey, Courtauld Institute of Art.

Fig. 21. "A Torchbearer: An Oceania," one of Inigo Jones's watercolour costume designs for *The Masque of Blackness*. Devonshire Collection, Chatsworth. Reproduced by permission of the Duke of Devonshire and the Trustees of the Chatsworth Settlement. Photograph: Photographic Survey, Courtauld Institute of Art.

have come on their quest through Mauretania, Lusitania, and Aquitania without success. The talking reflection turns out to have been the African moon goddess, Aethiopia, who suddenly appears on stage in another Jonesian *coup de théâtre* and proclaims to Niger that they have indeed found the glorious land they seek: Britannia, "[r]uled by a sun ... / Whose beams shine day and night and are of force / To blanch an Ethiop, and revive a corse." The Tritons sound their horns, a dance ensues, and the masquers formally present themselves, each displaying her allegorical name and hieroglyphic symbol. Aethiopia assures them that after a year here, bathed by the ocean and blanched by the beams of "yond' bright sun" (that same King James whose power can revivify the dead), they will attain the "perfection"—the whiteness—they seek. This resolution, to have been effected in a sequel masque the following Twelfth Night, had to wait yet another two years until 1608 when *The Masque of Beauty* was finally produced. Music, singing, and more dancing conclude *The Masque of Blackness* which, Orgel points out, may have taken three hours to perform, even though its text is only about eleven pages long (113).

Critical readings of this masque have generally focused on the symbolic qualities of blackness (Orgel 121–28) and its allegorical systems of meaning derived by Jonson from Italian neo-Platonist manuals (Gordon 134–56). But in recent years some critics have insisted on understanding *The Masque of Blackness* more literally in feminist and postcolonial terms of gender, race, and politics. Hardin Aasand reads the masque as "a mimetic document of Queen Anne's marginal existence in the Jacobean court" (271). For Kim F. Hall, "[t]he twin concerns of patriarchy and imperialism meet ... with the actual blackness encountered in the quest for empire" (5). She sees King James's efforts to create a united Great Britain (the "new name" of Britannia) "continually yoked to the glorification of whiteness" in the masque (9). Hall concludes that "*The Masque of Blackness* presents an idealized world in which normally intransigent blackness is subdued by a European order predicated on white, male privilege and power" (12). Yumna Siddiqi positions the masque in the context of the burgeoning slave trade and anxieties around the growing presence of Africans in England. She reads the lines in the opening song regarding "the orient flood / Into the west" as a reference to the incursion of "fluid and uncontrolled" African bodies (although "orient" would probably not have been understood at the time to include "African"), and she argues that, "at the same time, the productive capacity of the African body is a potential asset to Britain. The control of this labor is the ideological project of the masque" (143–45). Lesley Mickel synthesizes all these readings, proposing that the masque addresses issues of gender, colour, and race "in relation to a nascent imperialism, while exhorting James to become … the ideal ruler of an emerging British empire" (47). Mickel makes the case that *The Masque of Blackness*, and Jonson's writings for the court generally, contributed to "the evolution of an imperial discourse that held sway well into the twentieth century, whereby British imperial occupation was seen to entail educational and cultural improvement for the new world, whose subjects were moulded according to a British pattern, thereby becoming 'white' in outlook although not in skin colour" (49–50).

One need not fully embrace these points of view to see the "nascent imperialism" of an emerging colonial power at least foreshadowed, if not reflected, in *The Masque of Blackness*. Reading history back into these works—carefully and accurately, one hopes—helps to revitalize a theatrical form that, for many of us, has long seemed effete and outdated. Like Lescarbot, Jonson insisted that his ephemeral masque be recorded for access by his contemporaries who would not have been present at the performance, as well as for posterity, and both arranged for their works' publication as soon as possible after their productions. Not just the hope of literary fame but history itself weighed on them both—the history of their own age, sure to be a Golden Age, graced by all the gods, incarnated in these spectacles of imperial aggrandizement.

The Masque of Blackness

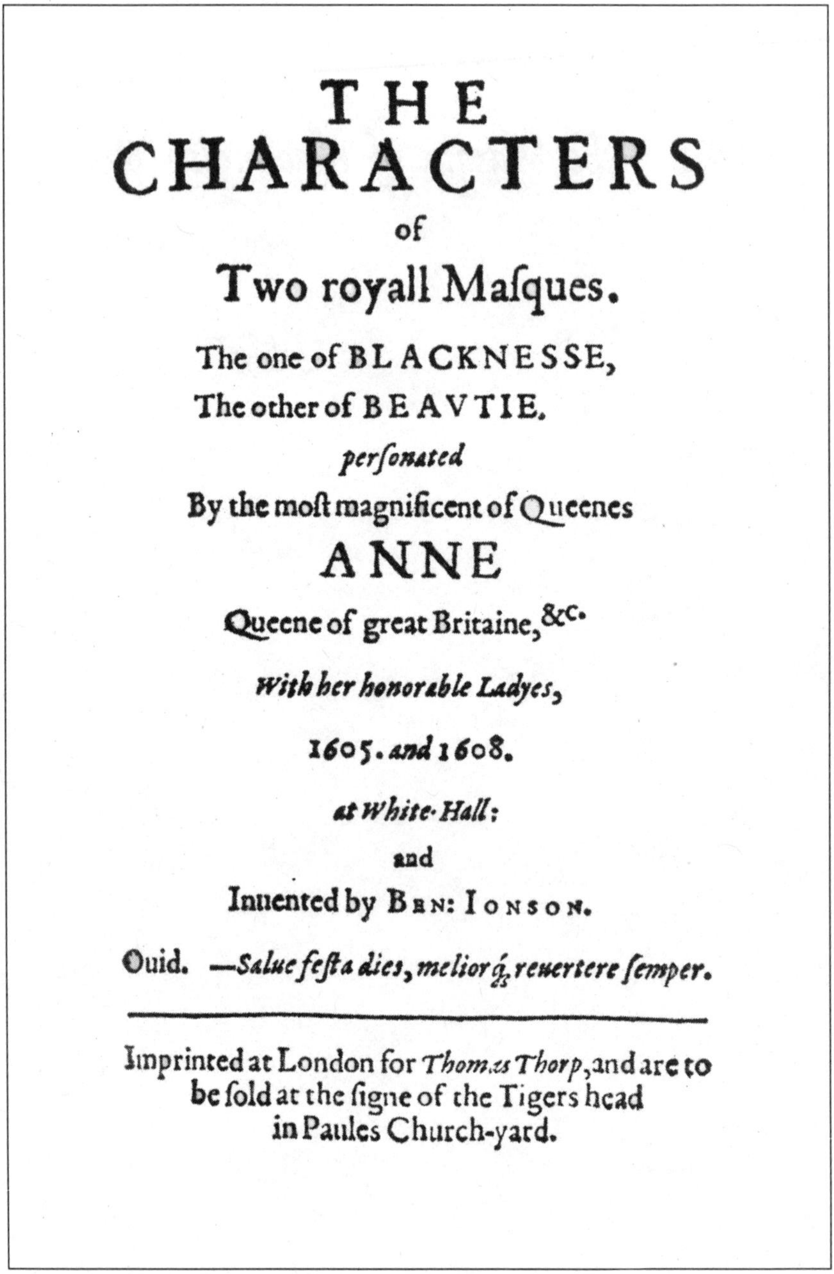

THE
CHARACTERS

of

Two royall Mafques.

The one of BLACKNESSE,
The other of BEAVTIE.

perfonated

By the moft magnificent of Queenes

ANNE

Queene of great Britaine, &c.

with her honorable Ladyes,

1605. and 1608.

at White-Hall:

and

Inuented by BEN: IONSON.

Ouid. —*Salue fefta dies, meliorq̄, reuertere femper.*

Imprinted at London for *Thomas Thorp*, and are to
be fold at the figne of the Tigers head
in Paules Church-yard.

Fig. 22. Title page of the 1608 Quarto publication of *The Masques of Blackness* and *of Beauty*.

The Masque of Blackness

Ben Jonson (1605)

The Queen's Masques
The first, of BLACKNESS

Personated at the court at Whitehall on the Twelfth Night, 1605.

The honour and splendour of these spectacles was such in the performance as, could those hours have lasted, this of mine now had been a most unprofitable work. But, when it is the fate even of the greatest and most absolute births to need and borrow a life of posterity, little had been done to the study of magnificence in these if presently with the rage of the people, who, as a part of greatness, are privileged by custom to deface their carcasses, the spirits had also perished. In duty, therefore, to that Majesty who gave them their authority and grace, and, no less than the most royal of predecessors, deserves eminent celebration for these solemnities, I add this later hand to redeem them as well from ignorance as envy, two common evils, the one of censure, the other of oblivion.

Pliny, Solinus, Ptolemy, and of late Leo the African, remember unto us a river in Ethiopia famous by the name of Niger, of which the people were called *Nigritae*, now Negroes, and are the blackest nation of the world. This river taketh spring out of a certain lake, eastward, and after a long race falleth into the western ocean. Hence (because it was her Majesty's will to have them blackamoors at first), the invention was derived by me, and presented thus.

First, for the scene, was drawn a Landscape consisting of small woods, and here and there a void place filled with huntings; which falling, an artificial sea was seen to shoot forth, as if it flowed to the land, raised with waves which seemed to

*move, and in some places the billow to break, as imitating that orderly disorder
which is common in nature. In front of this sea were placed six Tritons in moving
and sprightly actions, their upper parts human, save that their hairs were blue, as
partaking of the sea colour, their desinent[1] parts fish, mounted above their heads,
and all varied in disposition. From their backs were borne out certain light pieces
of taffeta as if carried by the wind, and their music made out of wreathed shells.
Behind these a pair of sea-maids, for song, were as conspicuously seated; between
which two great sea-horses (as big as the life) put forth themselves, the one
mounting aloft and writhing his head from the other, which seemed to sink
forwards (so intended for variation, and that the figure behind might come off
better). Upon their backs Oceanus and Niger were advanced.*

*Oceanus, presented in a human form, the colour of his flesh blue, and shadowed
with a robe of sea-green; his head grey and horned, as he is described by the
ancients; his beard of the like mixed colour. He was garlanded with algae, or sea-
grass, and in his hand a trident.*

*Niger, in form and colour of an Ethiop, his hair and rare beard curled,
shadowed with a blue and bright mantle; his front, neck and wrists adorned with
pearl; and crowned with an artificial wreath of cane and paper-rush.[2]*

*These induced[3] the masquers, which were twelve nymphs, Negroes, and the
daughters of Niger, attended by so many of the Oceaniae, which were their light-
bearers.*

*The masquers were placed in a great concave shell like mother of pearl, curiously
made to move on those waters and rise with the billow; the top thereof was stuck
with a chevron of lights which, indented to the proportion of the shell, struck a
glorious beam upon them as they were seated one above another; so that they were
all seen, but in an extravagant order.*

*On sides of the shell did swim six huge sea-monsters, varied in their shape and
dispositions, bearing on their backs the twelve torch-bearers, who were planted
there in several greces,[4] so as the backs of some were seen, some in profile, or side,
others in face; and all having their lights burning out of whelks or murex shells.*

*The attire of the masquers was alike in all, without difference; the colours,
azure and silver; their hair thick and curled upright in tresses, like pyramids, but
returned on the top with a scroll and antique dressing of feathers and jewels
interlaced with ropes of pearl. And for the front, ear, neck and wrists, the ornament
was of the most choice and orient pearl, best setting off from the black.*

*For the light-bearers, sea-green, waved about the skirts with gold and silver;
their hair loose and flowing, garlanded with sea-grass, and that stuck with
branches of coral.*

---

1. DESINENT – lower.   2. PAPER-RUSH – papyrus.   3. INDUCED – led in.   4. GRECES – steps.

These thus presented, the scene behind seemed a vast sea, and united with this that flowed forth, from the termination or horizon of which (being the level of the state, which was placed in the upper end of the hall) was drawn, by the lines of perspective, the whole work shooting downwards from the eye; which decorum made it more conspicuous, and caught the eye afar off with a wandering beauty. To which was added an obscure and cloudy night-piece that made the whole set off. So much for the bodily part, which was of Master Inigo Jones his design and act.

By this, one of the Tritons, with the two sea-maids, began to sing to[5] *the others' loud music, their voices being a tenor and two trebles.*[6]

SONG

Sound, sound aloud
The welcome of the orient flood
Into the west;
Fair Niger, son to great Oceanus,
Now honoured thus
With all his beauteous race,
Who, though but black in face,
Yet are they bright,
And full of life and light,
To prove that beauty best
Which not the colour but the feature
Assures unto the creature.

OCEANUS

Be silent now the ceremony's done,
And Niger, say, how comes it, lovely son,
That thou, the Ethiop's river, so far east,
Art seen to fall into th'extremest west
Of me, the king of floods, Oceanus,
And in mine empire's heart salute me thus?
My ceaseless current now amazèd stands
To see thy labour through so many lands
Mix thy fresh billow with my brackish stream,
And in thy sweetness stretch thy diadem
To these far distant and unequalled skies,
This squarèd circle of celestial bodies.[7]

---

5. SING TO – harmonize with. 6. TREBLES – sopranos. 7. SQUARÈD CIRCLE ... BODIES – heavenly bodies perfectly transformed into the earthly.

NIGER

Divine Oceanus, 'tis not strange at all
That, since the immortal souls of creatures mortal
Mix with their bodies, yet reserve forever
A power of separation, I should sever
My fresh streams from thy brackish, like things fixed,
Though with thy powerful saltness thus far mixed.
"Virtue, though chained to earth, will still live free,
And hell itself must yield to industry."

OCEANUS

But what's the end of thy Herculean labours,
Extended to these calm and blessèd shores?

NIGER

To do a kind and careful father's part,
In satisfying every pensive heart
Of these my daughters, my most lovèd birth:
Who, though they were the first formed dames of earth,
And in whose sparkling and refulgent eyes
The glorious sun did still delight to rise;
Though he (the best judge and most formal cause
Of all dames' beauties) in their firm hues draws
Signs of his fervent'st love, and thereby shows
That in their black the perfect'st beauty grows,
Since the fixed colour of their curlèd hair
(Which is the highest grace of dames most fair)
No cares, no age can change, or there display
The fearful tincture of abhorrèd grey,
Since Death herself (herself being pale and blue)
Can never alter their most faithful hue;
All which are arguments to prove how far
Their beauties conquer in great beauty's war,
And more, how near divinity they be
That stand from passion or decay so free.
Yet since the fabulous voices of some few
Poor brain-sick men, styled poets here with you,
Have with such envy of their graces sung

The painted beauties other empires sprung,
Letting their loose and wingèd fictions fly
To infect all climates, yea, our purity;
As of one Phaëton,[8] that fired the world,
And that before his heedless flames were hurled
About the globe, the Ethiops were as fair
As other dames, now black with black despair;
And in respect of their complexions changed,
Are eachwhere, since, for luckless creatures ranged.
Which when my daughters heard (as women are
Most jealous of their beauties), fear and care
Possessed them whole; yea, and believing them,
They wept such ceaseless tears into my stream
That it hath thus far overflowed his shore
To seek them patience; who have since e'ermore
As the sun riseth charged his burning throne
With volleys of revilings, 'cause he shone
On their scorched cheeks with such intemperate fires,
And other dames made queens of all desires.
To frustrate which strange error oft I sought,
Though most in vain, against a settled thought
As women's are, till they confirmed at length
By miracle what I with so much strength
Of argument resisted; else they feigned:
For in the lake where their first spring they gained,
As they sat cooling their soft limbs one night,
Appeared a face all circumfused with light
(And sure they saw't, for Ethiops never dream)
Wherein they might decipher through the stream
These words:
    That they a land must forthwith seek
    Whose termination (of the Greek)
    Sounds -*tania*; where bright Sol, that heat
    Their bloods, doth never rise or set,
    But in his journey passeth by,
    And leaves that climate of the sky
    To comfort of a greater light,
    Who forms all beauty with his sight.

---

8. PHAËTON – son of the sun god Apollo.

In search of this have we three princedoms passed
That speak out -*tania* in their accents last:
Black Mauretania[9] first, and secondly
Swarth Lusitania;[10] next we did descry
Rich Aquitania,[11] and yet cannot find
The place unto these longing nymphs designed.
Instruct and aid me, great Oceanus,
What land is this that now appears to us?

OCEANUS

This land that lifts into the temperate air
His snowy cliff is Albion the fair,
So called of Neptune's son, who ruleth here;
For whose dear guard, myself four thousand year,
Since old Deucalion's[12] days, have walked the round
About his empire, proud to see him crowned
Above my waves.

At this the moon was discovered in the upper part of the house, triumphant in a silver throne made in figure of a pyramid. Her garments white and silver, the dressing of her head antique, and crowned with a luminary, or sphere of light, which striking on the clouds, and heightened with silver, reflected as natural clouds do by the splendour of the moon. The heaven about her was vaulted with blue silk and set with stars of silver which had in them their several lights burning. The sudden sight of which made Niger to interrupt Oceanus with this present passion.

NIGER

O see, our silver star!
Whose pure, auspicious light greets us thus far!
Great Aethiopia, goddess of our shore,
Since with particular worship we adore
Thy general brightness, let particular grace
Shine on my zealous daughters; show the place
Which long their longings urged their eyes to see.
Beautify them, which long have deified thee.

---

9. MAURETANIA – The Land of the Moors, North Africa. 10. LUSITANIA – Portugal and western Spain. 11. AQUITANIA - southwestern France. 12. DEUCALION – a Greek Noah, survivor of a great flood.

AETHIOPIA

Niger, be glad; resume thy native cheer.
Thy daughters' labours have their period[13] here,
And so thy errors. I was that bright face
Reflected by the lake, in which thy race
Read mystic lines (which skill Pythagoras
First taught to men by a reverberate glass).[14]
This blessèd isle doth with that -*tania* end,
Which there they saw inscribed, and shall extend
Wished satisfaction to their best desires.
Britannia, which the triple world[15] admires,
The isle hath now recovered for her name;
Where reign those beauties that with so much fame
The sacred muses' sons have honourèd,
And from bright Hesperus to Eos[16] spread.
With that great name Britannia, this blest isle
Hath won her ancient dignity and style,
A world divided from the world, and tried
The abstract[17] of it in his general pride.
For were the world with all his wealth a ring,
Britannia, whose new name makes all tongues sing,
Might be a diamond worthy to enchase[18] it,
Ruled by a sun that to this height doth grace it,
Whose beams shine day and night, and are of force
To blanch an Ethiop, and revive a corse.
His light sciential is, and (past mere nature)
Can salve the rude defects of every creature.
    Call forth thy honoured daughters, then,
    And let them, 'fore the Britain men,
    Indent the land with those pure traces[19]
    They flow with, in their native graces.
    Invite them boldly to the shore,
    Their beauties shall be scorched no more;
    This sun is temperate, and refines
    All things on which his radiance shines.

---

13. PERIOD – conclusion.   14. PYTHAGORAS … GLASS – Pythagoras was supposedly able to write messages onto the moon with a "reverberate," a reflecting glass.   15. TRIPLE WORLD – heaven, earth, and the underworld.   16. HESPERUS TO EOS – evening to dawn, west to east.   17. TRIED / THE ABSTRACT – experienced the ideal image.   18. ENCHASE – set in.   19. TRACES – footsteps.

Here the Tritons sounded, and they danced on shore, every couple as they advanced severally presenting their fans, in one of which were inscribed their mixed names, in the other a mute hieroglyphic expressing their mixed qualities. Which manner of symbol I rather chose than imprese,[20] *as well for strangeness as relishing of antiquity, and more applying to that original doctrine of sculpture which the Egyptians are said first to have brought from the Ethiopians.*

	The names	The symbols
The Queen Countess of Bedford	*Euphoris*[21] *Aglaia*[22]	A golden tree laden with fruit.
Lady Herbert Countess of Derby	*Diaphane*[23] *Eucampse*[25]	The figure icosahedron[24] of crystal.
Lady Rich Countess of Suffolk	*Ocyte*[26] *Kathare*[27]	A pair of naked feet in a river.
Lady Bevill Lady Effingham	*Notis*[28] *Psychrote*[29]	The salamander simple.
Lady Elizabeth Howard Lady Susan de Vere	*Glycyte*[30] *Malacia*[31]	A cloud full of rain, dropping.
Lady Wroth Lady Walsingham	*Baryte*[32] *Periphere*[33]	An urn, sphered with wine.

The names of the Oceaniae were

Doris	*Cydippe*	*Beroe*	*Ianthe*
Petraea	*Glauce*	*Acaste*	*Lycoris*
Ocyrhoe	*Tyche*	*Clytia*	*Plexaure*

Their own single dance ended, as they were about to make choice of their men, one from the sea was heard to call 'em with this charm, sung by a tenor voice.

SONG

Come away, come away,
We grow jealous of your stay;
If you do not stop your ear,
We shall have more cause to fear

---

20. IMPRESE – emblems.   21. EUPHORIS – abundance.   22. AGLAIA – splendour.   23. DIAPHANE – transparency.   24. ICOSAHEDRON – a twenty-sided figure.   25. EUCAMPSE – flexibility.   26. OCYTE – swiftness.   27. KATHARE – spotlessness.   28. NOTIS – moisture.   29. PSYCHROTE – cold.   30. GLYCYTE – sweetness.   31. MALACIA – delicacy.   32. BARYTE – weight.   33. PERIPHERE – circularity.

Sirens of the land, than they
To doubt the sirens of the sea.

Here they danced with their men several measures and corantos.[34] *All which
ended, they were again accited*[35] *to sea with a song of two trebles, whose cadences
were iterated by a double echo from several parts of the land.*

SONG

Daughters of the subtle flood,
Do not let earth longer entertain you;
1st ECHO: Let earth longer entertain you.
2nd ECHO: Longer entertain you.
'Tis to them enough of good
That you give this little hope to gain you.
1st ECHO: Give this little hope to gain you.
2nd ECHO: Little hope to gain you.
If they love,
You shall quickly see;
For when to flight you move,
They'll follow you, the more you flee.
1st ECHO: Follow you, the more you flee.
2nd ECHO: The more you flee.
If not, impute it each to other's matter;
They are but earth,
1st ECHO: But earth.
2nd ECHO: Earth.
And what you vowed was water.
1st ECHO: And what you vowed was water.
2nd ECHO: You vowed was water.

AETHIOPIA

Enough, bright nymphs, the night grows old,
And we are grieved we cannot hold
You longer light; but comfort take.
Your father only to the lake
Shall make return; yourselves, with feasts,
Must here remain the Ocean's guests.
Nor shall this veil the sun hath cast

---

34. CORANTOS – dances. 35. ACCITED – called.

Above your blood more summers last.
For which, you shall observe these rites:
Thirteen times thrice, on thirteen nights
(So often as I fill my sphere
With glorious light throughout the year),
You shall, when all things else do sleep
Save your chaste thoughts, with reverence steep
Your bodies in that purer brine
And wholesome dew called rosmarine.
Then with that soft and gentler foam,
Of which the ocean yet yields some,
Whereof bright Venus, beauty's queen,
Is said to have begotten been,
You shall your gentler limbs o'er-lave,
And for your pains perfection have.
So that, this night, the year gone round,
You do again salute this ground,
And in the beams of yond' bright sun
Your faces dry, and all is done.

At which, in a dance they returned to the sea, where they took their shell, and with this full song went out.

SONG

Now Dian[36] with her burning face
Declines apace,
By which our waters know
To ebb, that late did flow.
Back seas, back nymphs, but with a forward[37] grace
Keep, still, your reverence to the place;
And shout with joy of favour you have won
In sight of Albion, Neptune's son.

So ended the first masque, which (beside the singular grace of music and dances) had that success in the nobility of performance as nothing needs to the illustration but the memory by whom it was personated.

❧

---

36. DIAN – the moon.   37. FORWARD – eager.

❧ Bibliography ❧

Bibliography

Aasand, Hardin. "'To Blanch an Ethiop, and Revive a Corse': Queen Anne and *The Masque of Blackness*." *Studies in English Literature, 1500–1900* 32 (Spring 1992): 271–85.

Armstrong, Joe C. W. *Champlain*. Toronto: Macmillan, 1987.

Atwood, Margaret. *Survival: A Thematic Guide to Canadian Literature*. Toronto: Anansi, 1972.

Barish, Jonas A. *Ben Jonson and the Language of Prose Comedy*. New York: Norton, 1970.

Baudry, René. "Lescarbot, Marc." *Dictionary of Canadian Biography Online*. 2000. http://www.biographi.ca/EN/ShowBio.asp?BioId=34473.

Benson, Eugene. "Marc Lescarbot and 'The Theatre of Neptune.'" *Canadian Drama* 8.1 (1982): 84–85.

Bergeron, David M. *English Civic Pageantry, 1558–1642*. London: Edward Arnold, 1971.

Biggar, H. P. "The French Hakluyt: Marc Lescarbot of Vervins." *American Historical Review* 6 (July 1901): 671–92.

Bowers, Rick. "*The Theatre of Neptune*: Marc Lescarbot and the New World Masque." *Canadian Drama* 15.1 (1989): 39–52.

Buisseret, David. *Henry IV*. London: George Allen and Unwin, 1984.

Ceremonial Entry of Ernst, Archduke of Austria, into Antwerp, June 14, 1594. Text by Johannes Bochius, engravings by Pieter van der Borcht, after designs by Marten de Vos. (1595) New York: Benjamin Blom, 1970.

"Champlain Anniversary." 23 June 2004. www.cbc.ca/news/background/champlainanniversary/.

Champlain, Samuel de. *The Voyages*. Trans. and ed. W. F. Ganong. In *The Works of Samuel de Champlain*. Vol. 1. Toronto: The Champlain Society, 1922. Reprint, Toronto: University of Toronto Press, 1971.

Davis, Peter A. "Plays and Playwrights to 1800." In Wilmeth and Bigsby, eds. 216–49.

Deloria, Philip J. *Playing Indian*. New Haven: Yale University Press, 1998.

Denison, Cara Dufour. *French Master Drawings from the Pierpont Morgan Library*. New York: Pierpont Morgan Library, 1993.

Doucette, Leonard E. *Theatre in French Canada: Laying the Foundations, 1606–1867*. Toronto: University of Toronto Press, 1984.

"Early American Literature (1609–1830)." The Harris Collection of American Poetry and Plays. John Hay Library, Brown University. www.brown.edu/Facilities/University_Library/collections/harris/Harris.EALit.html.

Emont, Bernard. *Marc Lescarbot: Mythes et rêves fondateurs de la Nouvelle-France*. Paris: L'Hamattan, 2002.

Filewod, Alan. *Performing Canada: The Nation Enacted in the Imagined Theatre*. Kamloops, B.C.: Textual Studies in Canada, 2002.

Fournier, Hannah. "Lescarbot's 'Théâtre de Neptune': New World Pageant, Old World Polemic." *Canadian Drama* 7.1 (Spring 1981): 3–11.

Francis, Daniel. *The Imaginary Indian: The Image of the Indian in Canadian Culture*. Vancouver: Arsenal Pulp Press, 1992.

Gardner, David. "An Analytical History of the Theatre in Canada: The European Beginnings to 1760." Ph.D. diss., University of Toronto, 1982.

———. "David Gardner Argues the Case for 1583." *Theatre History in Canada* 4 (Fall 1983): 226–37.

Gordon, D. J. *The Renaissance Imagination*. Ed. Stephen Orgel. Berkeley: University of California Press, 1975.

Hall, Kim F. "Sexual Politics and Cultural Identity in *The Masque of Blackness*." In *The Performance of Power: Theatrical Discourse and Politics*, ed. Sue-Ellen Case and Janelle Reinelt. Iowa City: University of Iowa Press, 1991. 3–18.

Jacob, Fred. "The Stage." *Canadian Forum* 7 (October 1926): 416.

Jacquot, Jean, ed. *Les Fêtes de la Renaissance I*. Paris: Centre National de la recherche scientifique, 1959.

———, and Elie Konigsen, eds. *Les Fêtes de la Renaissance III*. Paris: Centre National de la recherche scientifique, 1975.

Jefferys, Charles W. "The Reconstruction of the Port Royal Habitation of 1605–13." *Canadian Historical Review* 20 (December 1939): 368–77.

———. *The Picture Gallery of Canadian History*. Vol. 1. Toronto: Ryerson, 1942.

Jonson, Ben. *Ben Jonson* [works]. Ed. C. H. Herford and Percy and Evelyn Simpson. 11 vols. Oxford: Clarendon Press, 1925–52.

———. *The Masque of Blackness*. In *Ben Jonson: The Complete Masques*, ed. Stephen Orgel. New Haven: Yale University Press, 1969. 47–60.

———. *The Masque of Blackness*. In *Court Masques: Jacobean and Caroline Entertainments, 1605–1640*, ed. David Lindley. New York: Oxford University Press, 1995. 1–9, 215–18.

———. *The Masque of Blackness*. In *Ben Jonson's Plays and Masques*, ed. Richard Harp, 2nd ed. New York: Norton, 2001. 314–24.

King, Donovan. *Sinking Neptune*. 22 November 2005. http://optative.net/neptune/sinkingneptune.pdf.

Lescarbot, Marc. *The History of New France*. Trans. and ed. W. L. Grant. 3 vols. Toronto: Champlain Society, 1907–14. Reprint, New York: Greenwood Press, 1968.

———. *Le Théâtre de Neptune en la Nouvelle-France*. In *The History of New France*, ed. W. L. Grant. Vol. 3. 473–79.

———. *Nova Francia: A Description of Acadia, 1606*. Trans. P. Erondelle. 1609. New York: Harper and Brothers, 1928.

———. *Le Théâtre de Neptune*. Trans. R. K. Hicks. *Dalhousie Review* 34 (October 1926): 215–23.

———. *The Theatre of Neptune in New France*. Trans. Harriette Taber Richardson. Boston: Houghton Mifflin, 1927.

———. *The Theatre of Neptune in New France*. Trans. Eugene Benson and Renate Benson. *Canadian Drama* 8.1 (1982): 86–95. Reprinted in Wagner, ed. 35–43.

Litalien, Raymonde, and Denis Vaugeois, eds. *Champlain: The Birth of French America*. Trans. Käthe Roth. Montreal: Septentrion and McGill-Queen's University Press, 2004.

MacClintock, Carol. Introduction to *Le Balet Comique de la Royne 1581*. Trans. Carol and Lander MacClintock. Musicological Studies and Documents, no. 25. New York: American Institute of Musicology, 1971. 9–22.

McConachie, Bruce A. "Using the Concept of Cultural Hegemony to Write Theatre History." In *Interpreting the Theatrical Past: Essays in the Historiography of Performance*, ed. Thomas Postlewait and Bruce A. McConachie. Iowa City: University of Iowa Press, 1989. 37–58.

McGowan, Margaret C. "Form and Themes in Henri II's Entry into Rouen." In *Essays Principally on Masques and Entertainments*, ed. S. Schoenbaum. *Renaissance Drama*, New Series, no. 1. Evanston, Ill.: Northwestern University Press, 1968. 199–251.

Mickel, Lesley. *Ben Jonson's Antimasques: A History of Growth and Decline*. Aldershot: Ashgate, 1999.

Mielke, Hans. "Ceremonial Entries and the Theatre in the Sixteenth Century." In *Ceremonial Entry of Ernst, Archduke of Austria, into Antwerp, June 14, 1594*. VII–XXIII.

Miller, J. R. *Skyscrapers Hide the Heavens: A History of Indian-White Relations in Canada*. 3rd ed. Toronto: University of Toronto Press, 2000.

Moureau, François. "American Aboriginals in the *Ballets de Cour* in Champlain's Time." In Litalien and Vaugeois, eds. 43–49.

Nichols, Glen. "Translations of Four *Réceptions* in the Tradition of Lescarbot and Company." *Theatre Research in Canada* 20 (Spring 1999): 69–120.

Orgel, Stephen. *The Jonsonian Masque*. Cambridge, Mass.: Harvard University Press, 1965.

———, and Roy Strong. *Inigo Jones: The Theatre of the Stuart Court*. Vol. 1. Los Angeles: University of California Press, 1973.

Richardson, Harriette Taber. Introduction to *The Theatre of Neptune in New France*, by Marc Lescarbot, trans. Richardson. ix–xx.

Roach, Joseph. *Cities of the Dead: Circum-Atlantic Performance.* New York: Columbia University Press, 1996.

Schechner, Richard. "From Ritual to Theater and Back: The Efficacy-Entertainment Braid." *Performance Theory,* rev. ed. New York: Routledge, 2003. 112–69.

Schmeisser, Barbara M. "The Port Royal Habitation—A 'Politically Correct' Reconstruction?" *Collections of the Royal Nova Scotia Historical Society* 44 (1996): 41–47. http://www.gov.ns.ca/nsarm/virtual/habitation/schmeisser.asp.

Siddiqi, Yumna. "Dark Incontinents: The Discourses of Race and Gender in Three Renaissance Masques." In *Renaissance Drama in an Age of Colonization,* ed. Mary Beth Rose. *Renaissance Drama,* New Series, no. 23. Evanston, Ill.: Northwestern University Press, 1992. 139–64.

Strong, Roy. *Art and Power: Renaissance Festivals 1450–1650.* Woodbridge, Suffolk: Boydell, 1984.

———. *Splendor at Court: Renaissance Spectacle and the Theatre of Power.* Boston: Houghton Mifflin, 1973.

Thierry, Eric. *Marc Lescarbot (vers 1570–1641): Un homme de plume au service de la Nouvelle-France.* Paris: Honoré Champion, 2001.

———. "Champlain and Lescarbot: An Impossible Friendship." In Litalien and Vaugeois, eds. 121–34.

Vivanti, Corrado. "Henry IV, The Gallic Hercules." *Journal of the Warburg and Courtauld Institutes* 30 (1967): 176–97.

Wagner, Anton, ed. *Colonial Quebec: French-Canadian Drama, 1606 to 1966.* Vol. 4 of *Canada's Lost Plays.* Toronto: CTR, 1982.

Wagner, Marie-France, and David Vaillancourt, eds. *Le Roi dans la ville: Anthologie des entrées royales dans les villes françaises de province (1615–1660).* Paris: Honoré Champion, 2001.

Wasserman, Jerry. "Where Were You in '52? Canadian Theatre on the Eve of Stratford." *Canadian Theatre Review* 114 (Spring 2003): 6–10.

Watanabe-O'Kelly, Helen. "Early Modern European Festivals—Politics and Performance, Event and Record." In *Court Festivals of the European Renaissance: Art, Politics and Performance,* ed. J. R. Mulryne and Elizabeth Goldring. Aldershot: Ashgate, 2002. 15–25.

Welsford, Enid. *The Court Masque.* Cambridge: Cambridge University Press, 1927.

Wilmeth, Don B., and Christopher Bigsby, eds. *Beginnings to 1870.* Vol. 1 of *The Cambridge History of American Theatre.* New York: Cambridge University Press, 1998.